# gnostic ARCHITECT

Emily

He laid hold

of the diverse fragments

of his accidental fate

and forged them into a whole—

a fictional whole,

it must be said.

Ernest Becker

*to*

# U R E

**Edited by Brad Collins and Elizabeth Zimmermann**

# gnostic
## ARCHITECT

ERIC OWEN MOSS

THE MONACELLI PRESS

to

URE

First published in the United States of America in 1999 by
The Monacelli Press, Inc.,
10 East 92nd Street, New York, New York 10128.

Copyright © 1999 by The Monacelli Press, Inc.

Library of Congress Cataloging-in-Publication Data
Moss, Eric Owen, 1943– .
Gnostic architecture / Eric Owen Moss.
p. cm.
1. Moss, Eric Owen, 1943– . 2. Architecture—Philosophy. I. Title.
NA737.M73A4  1998                               98-42479
720'.1—dc21

Printed and bound in Singapore

DESIGN AND COMPOSITION BY

Group C Inc NEW HAVEN/BOSTON

(BC, FS, CW, EZ)

# CONTENTS

know

# I
# OUTSIDE $\frac{OF}{THE}$ OUTSIDE

## 1.1

"My name is Ozymandias, king of kings:
 Look on my works, ye Mighty, and despair!"
 Nothing beside remains.
 Round the decay
 Of that colossal wreck, boundless and bare,
 The lone and level sands stretch far away.[1]

The works are gone, along with the king of kings. Cities are cemeteries, in a certain sense. I once had an astonishing photo of the outside corner of Crown Hall at IIT. The corner of the building was overgrown with vines, completely invisible, not the ideological abstraction Mies van der Rohe conceived. Two perspectives: one, the irrepressible capacity of architecture to change, momentum to build, culture by culture, culture over culture, in perpetuity; two, only the vines remain, devouring everything underneath. Where did that perpetual metamorphosis go? Somehow the engine continues. Go to Venice,[2] a city conceived by a draconian cast of the most diabolical characters. Feel it again—the colossal energy. Perhaps the Doge's Palace should have been round and blue, but it's the Doge's Palace anyway—it's there. Not always what you love, but always moving on—architecture breathing. If, as a by-product, a few bodies were dumped in the Grand Canal, those who survived powered the city. And the city powered its inhabitants. Remarkable civic constructions have been built in myriad places over millennia. An unseen force propels these endless acts of invention and reinvention—and their demise. We have to be conscious of architecture rising and falling.

## 1.2    Architecture may have no need of past histories if buildings can document their own internal history. The past sends along messages, and the loudest at the advent of modernism was the

Montage. Samitaur site, before construction, 1987.
1. Percy Bysshe Shelley, "Ozymandias," 1817.
2. Map of Venice, Italy.

unadulterated adulation of the technological prowess that changed the balance of a contest that had gone on between little human and big nature since Neolithic times. The residents of Chauvet, Lascaux, and Altamira[3] were often terrified because the world, as they experienced it, was so far beyond their capacity to manage. Cultures have had to protect themselves from the great Unmanageable, and have consistently invented exegeses in their attempt to account for why the world is as it is—whether it's Nazca[4] in the Peruvian highlands, or James the Just in Jerusalem, or Buddha with his hand on the ground.

And then modern technology arrived and said, "Wait a minute. We can control the weather, and explain the surface of the moon and the tides and what's at the center of the Earth. We can heat the houses and light the streets and travel the city in automobiles. We're in control." It seemed to be the end of a thirty-thousand-year run. Modern culture moved from defense to offense. There's a promotional chorus

3. See 3.3.
4. See 3.21.

about the ultimate significance of all these advances, big and little—electric pencil sharpeners, mini-recorders, multiple-line phones, fiber optics, computers, and the Internet—how they provide information and create jobs and make money. **What ephemeral presumptions is all of that sitting on?**

Too much "techno" cheerleading of the early modernist era, with Sigfried Giedion beating the band. I can appreciate the energy and enthusiasm; but that approach seems less sophisticated now. The early modern cheerleading outran its depth. And the self-confidence turned to arrogance. The moderns, at that point, no longer understood themselves as both separate from, and part of, a continuum that metamorphoses perpetually. I participated in a symposium at the Royal Academy several years ago, and a colleague got up and said, "My language is the language of the architecture of the twenty-first century." The vanity of the avant-garde outruns its ability to understand its own limits. It's not that the vanity *shouldn't* exist, or that the talent *doesn't* exist, or that the insight *can't* exist—but it often runs away with the advocate. Into a wall. **A paradigm has to include a suspicion of itself.**

1.3  Gnostic architecture is autobiographical. The thesis originates in my efforts over a number of years to provide an explanation for the world in which I (strangely) find myself. The intention is to avoid any dependence on questions of technique or technology. I am not concerned with accounting for building as a consequence of site circumstances. The process of developing the Gnostic argument requires stripping away every kind of empirical dependency that has been previously used to explain why buildings are what buildings are.

Gnostic architecture is not about faith in a movement, a methodology, a process, a technique, or a technology. It is a strategy for keeping architecture in a perpetual state of motion. That requires a certain self-confidence. One doesn't have to align oneself with the New Urbanists or the Deconstructivists or the Neominimalists. Those arguments, simply put, miss the point that there are always useful contradictory points. The Gnostic idea comes from a definition of Gnosis as a way of knowing that subsumes the contradictions of empirical knowledge—a (tenuously) complete knowing, arrived at personally. Internally. Person by person, one person at a time.

1.4   I'm trying to free myself from any method of thinking about architecture that provides the conclusion a priori. I'm looking for a way that doesn't preclude finally eliminating the way itself. Contemporary architects have often felt obligated to demonstrate a chronology of building logic without acknowledging what underlies that logic: "It was necessary to make a beam with a long horizontal end, because as it rotates, the span varies, and the column must support the beam at any point over this horizontal length." So it's okay? It's rational. It's logical, like the hypothetical MIT-imposed grid on

the moon's surface[5] that makes the moon intelligible (from the scientist's vantage point). I am looking for an argued chronology in which consistency is variable—the relationship of the columns to the girders, to the hidden steel, to the not-hidden steel, to the stiffeners perpendicular to the web, to the stiffeners parallel to the beams. Logic doesn't guarantee any truth outside its own premises. And many intriguing truths are not answerable to empirical logic. This reminds me of Degas's dancer:[6] looking for a balanced imbalance. In that crucible is the truth of the girder/column space at Samitaur. I'm looking for that stress. Only that tension between possibilities accurately represents our culture to itself.

1.5    You can't forget. The voice, the Gnostic voice, requires both an intelectual dialectic and a lyrical resolution. The dialectic locates the tension. The lyric subsumes it. The process of making a building is the process of making that cerebral subject matter tangible as the experience of the building. If you can sense that contradictory quality instinctively, without necessarily dealing with it in an intellectual way, then it's there. It's not so much that a particular rationale would validate the project, but that the project is validated by rendering the dialectic so sharply, so incisively, that a transcendent lyrical experience becomes available in the architecture. That sense of overcoming intellectual contradiction has to be present, or the architecture fails.

Architecture can't belong simply to an amalgamation of interests that serve the political or economic or social or utilitarian objectives of particular groups, however these necessities sort themselves out on the extroverted side of architecture. The question is always to what extent those extroverted interests are omnipotent, and to what extent they are actually more piecemeal, less homogeneous, and malleable enough to be adjusted to represent other, introverted, human qualities that are as real but more fragile and difficult to uncover. Those precarious qualities need to be precisely enunciated, insisted upon where they can be. They have to be protected over time—whether in monasteries, songs, or buildings. Architecture shouldn't ratify a consensus view of what's real. It should suggest an alternative. It should rearrange the consensus.

1.6    I became interested in Henry Moore's *Helmet*[7] in the last few years. It seemed to confirm some of my thinking about making space. A helmet, in a conventional sense, is readily understood. You put it on. It protects the

5. See 3.20 (Moon Map).
6. Edgar Degas, *Ballet Rehearsal*, 1876. See also 3.11.
7. Henry Moore, sketch for *Helmet*, 1939. See also 3.15.

head, acknowledging space for nose, mouth, ears, eyes, and the shape of the head. So head form and helmet form are essentially congruent. They ratify one another. But for Moore, what is contained within is not synonymous with the shape of the container; what is contained remains circumscribed by the container. What is inside is perceived from the outside through the holes but never complete-

ly understood. And there are areas of discontinuity of shape, disjunctions between container and contained. I analyze *Helmet* as a sequence of zones—the outside of the outside, the inside of the outside, the outside of the inside, and the inside of the inside. The tension, the "glue," is what I call the space between the inside of the outside and the outside of the inside. At Crown Hall,[8] Mies designed a block containing the main archi-

tecture building space, then placed a truss structure on top of the block. The position of the block confirms the position of the trusses and vice versa, just like the conventional helmet/head relationship. The two elements, block and trusses, confirm one another quite literally. I'm interested in the circumstance when two forms don't conform to one another but share enough of the congruent aspect to be read as both reinforcing and contradictory. **Fit and misfit.**

There's an intention to communicate this generic/specific dialectic in the Lawson/Westen House.[9]

Designing the roof support (a very large curve in section), I used glue-laminated wood components on each end, joined to a parallel pair of steel webs in the center to construct the beams. The three pieces attach to form a theoretical roof shape extending from one beam end to the other. Physically, literally, the completed manifestation of the generic beam occurred only once in the project. That beam overhangs the entry door. The other beams exist only as pieces of the hypothetical whole, to suggest the prospect that there is always a larger conception than could be known at any particular beam moment. **The architecture would be conceptually incomplete if it were to represent itself as complete in every circumstance,** disingenuous if it repeated only a single vantage point or system consistently and predictably.

Another instance of my intention to communicate a complete spatial understanding using the pieces piecemeal, which in the aggregate would constitute a complete understanding, is found in an initial sketch

8. Mies van der Rohe, Crown Hall, Illinois Institute of Technology, Chicago, Illinois, 1956.
9. EOM, Lawson/Westen House, Brentwood, California, 1993.

for the Lawson/Westen kitchen. I reviewed the sketch with the client. We agreed to abandon the strategy. Then the sketch idea returned as a ghost in the building, **a delicate remnant of the early idea. I** remember the discussion: "Hey Eric, where did this come from?" "Well, it came from the building that's no longer there." It was a residual consequence of the earlier thinking, and it suggested a route that could have been taken. So **the building becomes not only what it is, but what it was and could have been. The making of space is indicative not only of a conclusion, but of the process of arriving at that conclusion.** It is certainly conceivable for a completed building to include none of that process. But I think architecture requires more than a regurgitation of the historical record of antecedent buildings. **A building should give back its own history.**

1.7     There are strong indications of considered avenues that remain incomplete but plausible in other projects as well: Tours Art Center and Museum, in the medieval section of the city of Tours; the Brewery in Vienna remade as offices, entertainment, and retail; the Plaza Vieja in Havana;[10] and the social housing of Gasometer D-4 in Vienna. All these projects recollect forward—backward to touch a recollection, forward to alter that recollection. Tours[11] and Havana exploit backward (historically) not reverentially, but in the sense that the psychological construction of a human being, and the collective ethos of a culture, run in both directions: back into memory and forward toward what might reshape memory. At Chichen Itzá,[12] a new temple is built over the old. Hagia Sophia is a church that becomes a mosque that becomes a church.

**To move forward architecturally I have to erase something that was previously present.** This is particularly true in Havana; I couldn't come reverentially to the Plaza Vieja and say "I love Spanish colonial architecture." I had to be prepared to contest the old plaza, but still acknowledge that it is part of a continuum—be conscious of each era's belief systems and their incompleteness. We can't master it all—**neither the arrogance of empirical progress nor the cynicism of retrogressive reverence will succeed.** So Havana became the Plaza Vieja Nueva.

10. EOM, Contemporary Arts Center, Tours, France, 1993.
11. Plaza Vieja, Havana, Cuba.
12. See 3.9.

1.6

In the Havana project there was a strong antecedent, a tradition of use for the plaza: festivals, religious celebrations, athletics, markets; and all these were retained in the proposed iteration.[13] The strategy was to sustain and intensify those uses, to imagine a tension between past and future that no architecture of allegiance to either could have delivered. So the Plaza Vieja was Spanish colonial: a style of columns, a shape of beams, a conception of light wells, roofs, and interior spaces dealt with climatically and organizationally, with a big arcade wrapped around. And the design conclusion included including the antecedents. Early modern architecture only went forward (as it imagined itself), jettisoning a presumed stodgy, aristocratic architectural pedigree that ran backward for hundreds of years, replacing it with the "burn the city every forty years" exuberance of Marinetti and an unabashed reverence for technical prowess.

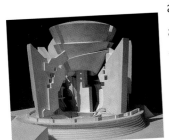

The new SAC project in Spain amends and significantly adds to an existing conception, this time on a site 1,500 by 400 meters. The Gasometer in Vienna[14] requires redefinition of a cylindrical, sixty-meter-diameter, end-of-the-nineteenth century natural gas tank near the airport. The project involved locating new housing, retail, and commercial facilities within the old tank while retaining the original masonry exterior wall. For the brewery in Vienna, the owner came to Los Angeles to look at our recent work. Our remaking of the industrial section of Los Angeles and

Culver City was a convincing precedent. A.R.City, the old freight train right-of-way in Culver City, belonged to a 1940s manufacturing and rail-delivery system in Los Angeles, developed on and around the Southern Pacific Railway track that ran through central Los Angeles. The A.R.City plan intentionally increases the building density and exacerbates the original railway line by inserting a series of high-density blocks over the old tracks.[15] All these projects catch history running in both directions.

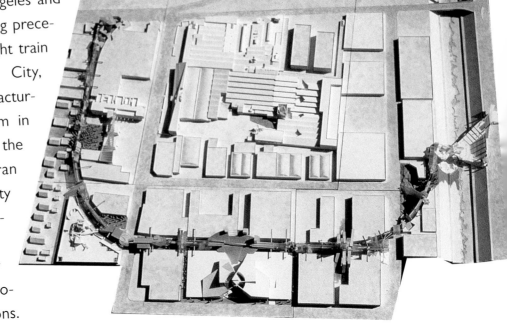

13. EOM, Plaza Nueva Vieja, Havana, Cuba, 1995.
14. EOM, Gasometer, Vienna, Austria, 1996. Top to bottom: proposed project, collage of model with existing walls, exterior with model of proposed project.
15. EOM, A.R.City, Culver City, California, 1991–1997. Model.

1.8     **All of a sudden, Samitaur rises.** There's no precedent for that building in Los Angeles—certainly not in the Baldwin Hills/La Cienega/Jefferson/South Central Los Angeles area. Virtually nothing has been built here recently—certainly nothing since the 1992 riots. For owners Frederick and Laurie Smith to bring a company like Kodak to the site is a great breakthrough for Los Angeles. New energy, new confidence, new jobs—all very contagious. And it has increased the prospect of construction for Samitaur 2 and Samitaur 3.

If you were to make a development proposal in Westwood in West Los Angeles, there would be hearings for five years, and perhaps never a built project. Developers and architects have to be very durable. I think the recent Culver City/Los Angeles projects have that durability. They are associated with the assumption that, after twelve years, the "nowhere" of La Cienega and Jefferson has now become a "somewhere." Somewhere only occurs where there are antecedents, but someone has to produce the first antecedent. We've done that with Samitaur. Perhaps, by example, the Samitaur project can refocus Los Angeles—adjust the vision of the city, the content of the city, the organization of the city, the vitality of the city, the collective prospect of the city.

1.9     The lesson of Moore's *Helmet*: Samitaur fits disparate pieces together—the legs, the stair, the pool, all of that. But they don't fit together by adjoining one another. The parts are intentional non sequiturs. Instead, all the shapes fit into something else, the glue, which allows them to cohere and become a building. The glue is a conceptual amoeba, delimited here by a mostly orthogonal perimeter—the Samitaur block and the attendant columns and girders necessary to lift it in the air. Then there are the four misfit exceptions—the entry stair anomaly, the pool/bridge anomaly, and the lounge and boardroom spaces.

**I couldn't design the building without an area of silence. Music everywhere doesn't work.** The music instinct implicates the frames underneath the Samitaur block.[16] Call it the music of the girders. There is a combination of intuition and method here that accounts for the rhythm and order of the steel parts. And it's complicated—placing columns behind existing walls in the original brick building so old piers and new columns almost coincide and the interior space is not disrupted; or, in the existing corrugated-steel building, placing new steel columns opposite old steel columns with a

16. Samitaur, view from underneath.

wall between so the relationship can be imagined but not seen. There are the large steel girders spanning the road—an essential organizer, a prototype, like a music staff for holding notes. But the girders are positioned variously, not consistently. The deep ends of the girders have a constant vertical relationship to the steel-pipe columns that support them. Each girder rotates its plan position, but the deepest section of the girder is always directly above the column. The small end of each girder has a varying horizontal position with respect to the column that supports it. And this second column might support the girder anywhere over the horizontal length of the short end. There are shear stiffeners on the girder face welded to the web. The stiffeners are arrayed based on two conditions: the shear forces in the girder, which decrease as the distance from the column increases; and the formal acknowledgment of a steel structure hidden in the soffit above. When there's a beam running above the girder (in the plaster soffit), not at right angles to that girder, the stiffener (normally perpendicular to the web) rotates to align with the hidden beam above. So the turned stiffener confirms the direction of the hidden steel presence.

The girder is always the same girder, but never the same girder. An understanding of the role of the stiffeners (always perpendicular, but not always perpendicular to the same plane) as they do and do not relate to a structural purpose was essential to the conception of the more conventional mutual obligations of the various components, which can become ever finer and more intricate.

The zinc finish on the girders is an example of that finer level of decision stiffeners, and pipe columns. The steel was cleaned, sprayed with zinc, and then hand-rubbed. The intention was that different workers would be rubbing different girders or portions of girders in different ways. So the technical description of the sprayed-zinc process is consistent, but the human hand makes the final result variable. So the girder finish is and is not consistent. If everything had been painted, then the paint would have homogenized the surface and taken away the individual hand. The general technical process and the personalized implementation process become one with the rubbed zinc. The zinc finish makes tangible the tension between general specifications and individual implementation and makes the dialectic intelligible.

What's the plaster color?[17] By intention it's a color you can't name. If you took the color components apart photochemically, you could say that some brown, some gray, some green, and some white would be found. Or you could say it's mostly green. All of these names could be recalled from the color chart in your head, but if you actually look at the color, you can't recognize it, and you don't know its name. You have to look. So you come to the experience of the

17. Samples of plaster finish. See also 5:4.

color with recollections of colors you have learned, and also confront something that you can't recall. Like the zinc color of the steel, the plaster color communicates the different hands that did the work. When we started applying the final color, I was standing on a scaffold and the plasterers were placing a mixture of colors on the wall and steel-troweling the plaster. We were discussing possibilities while the wet plaster was being applied. Each plasterer used slightly different amounts of pigment troweled in subtly different ways. But the degree of deviance had to be controlled. It was never "all of you characters get up on the scaffold and do whatever you want." The color of the building includes the person-by-person application nuance, in addition to the idea of the color that is no color you could name but only pieces of colors you thought you knew but now don't quite recognize in the Samitaur admixture.

1.10    The politicians ran way behind the project. Only when it arrived in the op-ed section of the *Times*, either *Times*, did the politicians start to pay attention. But now, with great energy, the staff of the mayor, consultants to the mayor, and the city planning department are helping us to expand the zoning possibilities, increase the height limits, and modify the parking and setback requirements. The city is anxious to change all the design criteria for the entire area. The key political operatives in the city who now find the project compelling had no associations with the project for ten years. Now La Cienega and Jefferson are becoming part of the mainstream discussion of planning in Los Angeles. The question is, **"Did the margin go to the center, or did the center go to the margin?"** That is, did a peripheral project modify itself sufficiently to be regarded as a sound development opportunity, or has the definition of sound opportunity been modified?

Neither architect nor developer began this project by accepting the conventional economic parameters for developing real estate as they stood in 1988. If you accepted those criteria in terms of the relative economic insignificance of the site, or the adjacency of the site to a perceived litany of social dangers, Samitaur would never have been built. All of the usual arguments that make new construction plausible were nonexistent, except the central location and the direct freeway access of the site. I've described the original site in contradictory ways—as a group of buildings that suggested amending, not bulldozing, and simultaneously as an opportunity to knock things down and start again.

If you look at the economic rationale, architecture quickly becomes irrelevant. That approach argues: access the key decision makers—the bankers, the politicians; find out where they're going, why they are going there; and join them. That was not our approach. If that had been the argument, we would have been working on Wilshire Boulevard instead of in central Los Angeles. The typical development argument is omitted from the Gnostic discussion. In a sense, it's there but it's inverted. Is it true that if you want to build, you have to play the big game with the big boys who make the big things happen? Under the guise of broadening the opportunity for architecture, this perspective actually limits the possibilities. It says, implicitly, that to build the architect must join the political and economic forces that implement work at a large scale. But what work? Maybe it depends on how long you (or they) are prepared to wait. Frederick and Laurie Smith's approach to this project in this area may be the behavioral exception that confirms the rule that a developer would never touch such a site, or it may be the exception that proves the exception doesn't have to remain an exception, but becomes the new rule.

1.11    The siting of the Samitaur block is, in part, a consequence of the a priori location of the road underneath, and the position of the two existing buildings that adjoin the road. That's not to say that the old buildings and the road automatically yield back the Samitaur building design. The project doesn't neatly read forward and backward in time. But there is an interrelationship between time backward and time forward on this site. Recollecting forward. The phrase matters. The idea matters. And it's not listed in the Los Angeles city zoning ordinance.

Ten years ago Frederick Smith came to me and said "I own a building on the site; it houses a tenant called Parties Plus; they don't have enough space. What can you do to increase their space within the existing sawtooth shed?" And I came back with the proposal for the block in the air over the road. The design process ran off and on for about ten years. In the L.A. City Building Department for preliminary review. Start. Stop. Working drawings. Start. Stop. And finally construction.

The position of the block depends upon the position of previous buildings on the site. It exists in the midst of those old structures but was not entirely proscribed by those now remodeled buildings. What explains the block? There was a service alley, not really quite a legitimate road. The alley was used by trucks, loading and off-loading from the sheds on either side of the road. The original, prac-tical arguments for lifting the building in the air were to maintain the truck use of the road and to sustain the manufacturing purposes of the buildings along the road.[18] But over the ten-year design process, the industrial uses essentially disappeared. They were no longer economically intelligible. There was a required fourteen-foot six-inch vertical clearance for trucks under the block; the Los Angeles

18. Drawing of Samitaur showing truck entry and egress.

Fire Department wouldn't allow the new building to extend over the old buildings below; and the L.A. city zoning ordinance limited the building height to three floors and forty-five feet. And yet, as perceptive and definitive as these criteria appear, they simply account for the theoretical perimeter of the block.

The building is as much an attitude toward city planning as it is a consequence of the site conditions. Constructing a piece of infrastructure like a freeway is not typically of much interest to a conventional owner/developer. As an urban image, Samitaur appears as a mechanism for superseding the regularized organization of buildings in Los Angeles. It is a supra-building—a bridge connecting many buildings. Discussion between architect and client: "We'll build the building over the road; we'll sustain and remodel the buildings adjacent to the road. Keep those uses going. Keep that money flowing. And meanwhile add a new building on top to alter the purpose of the site."

1.12　　　There should be a discussion of the meaning of the block in the air seen from a distance. No design details. Just the lifted 323-foot block as an element of infrastructure. As you get closer, the block becomes one of an infinite number of buildings in the area; it's both a single block and an ensemble of components. The outside of the outside is Samitaur from a distance, an addition to the city's infrastructure. It's a freeway. One hundred meters long, lifted in the air. By lifting the block on legs over the buildings that preceded it chronologically, it became supra-building-like, joining the infrastructure catalog list: freeway, concrete L.A. river, and myriad utility poles.

There was never a lot of interest on my part in a literal, detailed relationship of this building to the city, beyond the immediate site.[19] The block in the air is an analogue to its elevated freeway neighbor, the Santa Monica freeway to the north. They see each other: two hunks of freeway. On the adjacent site, two new high-rise buildings and a low-rise building are being designed. So the erstwhile industrial area is disappearing quickly. The Samitaur building is the progenitor of a new and renewed urban conception.

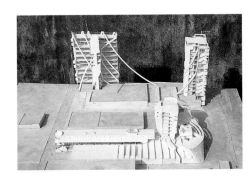

What is appealing about Samitaur 1, 2, and 3 (1, the built building; 2, the Hook and its evolution to the Hook and tower; 3, two 235-foot high-rise buildings)[20] is that, evaluated conventionally, it was hardly a remarkable design opportunity. Quite the opposite. **The site was nothing in the middle of nowhere. It was Bob Dylan singing "Desolation Row."** The area was on its way to petty crime, some gangs, a thriving co-op called Fedco down in the flats, and, up on a hill, middle-class, mostly black single-family housing at an (almost) safe distance from the riot territory (1965, 1992) of the flatlands. In addition, there was a forty-year accumulation of light industrial and manufacturing infrastructure, dying because those activities are now more affordable elsewhere.

We went into that area and reconstituted its life, transplanted its heart—pushing for a plausible, livable urban vision. Nobody but Frederick and Laurie Smith saw the opportunity. The L.A. city planning staff projected manufacturing in perpetuity, a color on a map, with limited heights and limited use. Our group saw an opportunity to reconstitute the central city area that was not, at that moment, politically sensitive to the pressures that constrain almost every project in every big American city now: vociferous, anti-building neighbors and their lawyers castigating every new project as the harbinger of massive traffic and pollution. Almost any individual can stop almost any project proposal today in America. It's not a coalescing of opinion that decides; it's the minority of the minority that very often governs. But no one seemed concerned enough to try to stop us in central Los Angeles or in industrial Culver City. The area, apparently, didn't matter much. So we were able to run a long way before anyone noticed that we were running at all. Who would run there? Certainly not the developers who foresee credible development only on Fifth Avenue, or Wilshire Boulevard, or Michigan

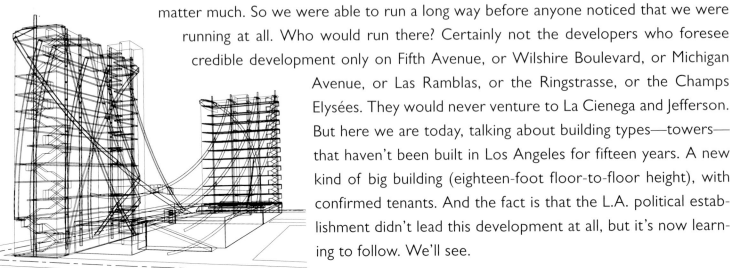

Avenue, or Las Ramblas, or the Ringstrasse, or the Champs Elysées. They would never venture to La Cienega and Jefferson. But here we are today, talking about building types—towers—that haven't been built in Los Angeles for fifteen years. A new kind of big building (eighteen-foot floor-to-floor height), with confirmed tenants. And the fact is that the L.A. political establishment didn't lead this development at all, but it's now learning to follow. We'll see.

20. Models and drawing showing Samitaur 2 and 3, 1997.

1.13   When you examine the streets, the tracks, the concrete drainage channel, the generic industrial sheds, See's Candy, Fedco, KABC, and Turner Broadcasting, they appear to be part of a complicated matrix of uses assembled over fifty or sixty years. But the originating purposes have dissipated and are about to disappear entirely. **The Samitaur building, though it belongs to the a priori site conditions that contributed to the conception of the block in the air over the old road, has instigated a new and radically different site organization.** The completion of Samitaur encouraged major revisions by the Los Angeles city planning department to the general plan guidelines for the Jefferson/La Cienega site. The revisions extend height limits from 45 to 235 feet, eliminate setbacks, and make parking and use requirements considerably more flexible. These changes have made possible the planning and design of three new buildings, substantially different in scale and purpose from what was allowed on the pre-Samitaur site. The enthusiasm for change in the city that Samitaur precipitated is the next story. I don't think that momentum was foreseen when Samitaur was designed. In completing the building, I came to understand that completion is always partial.

# 2
# INSIDE OF THE OUTSIDE

2.3

2.7

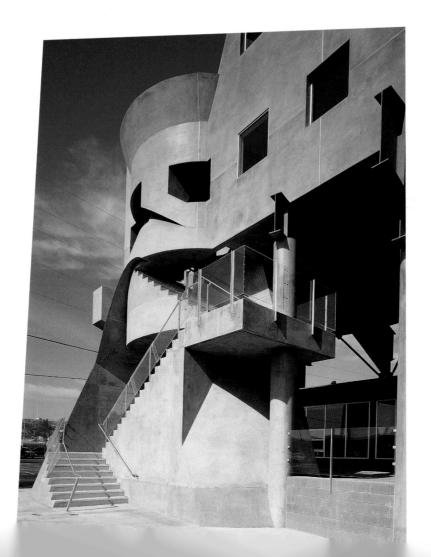

2.13

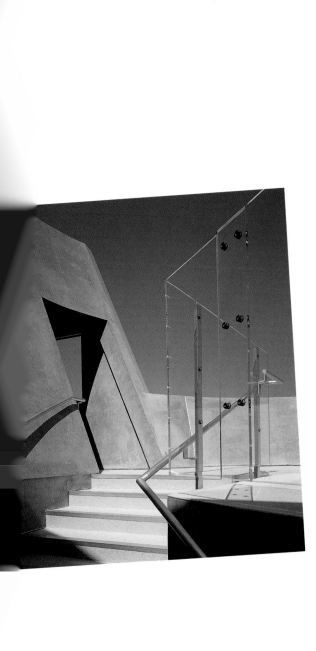

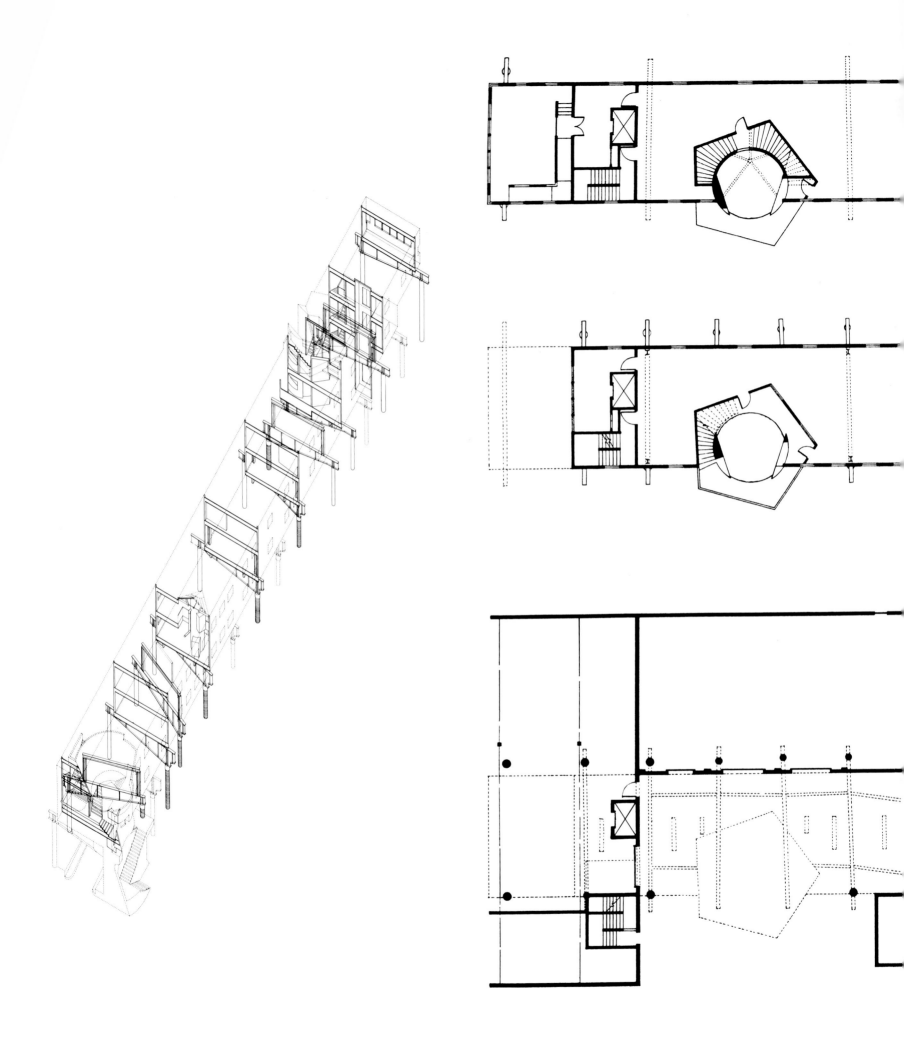

2.21

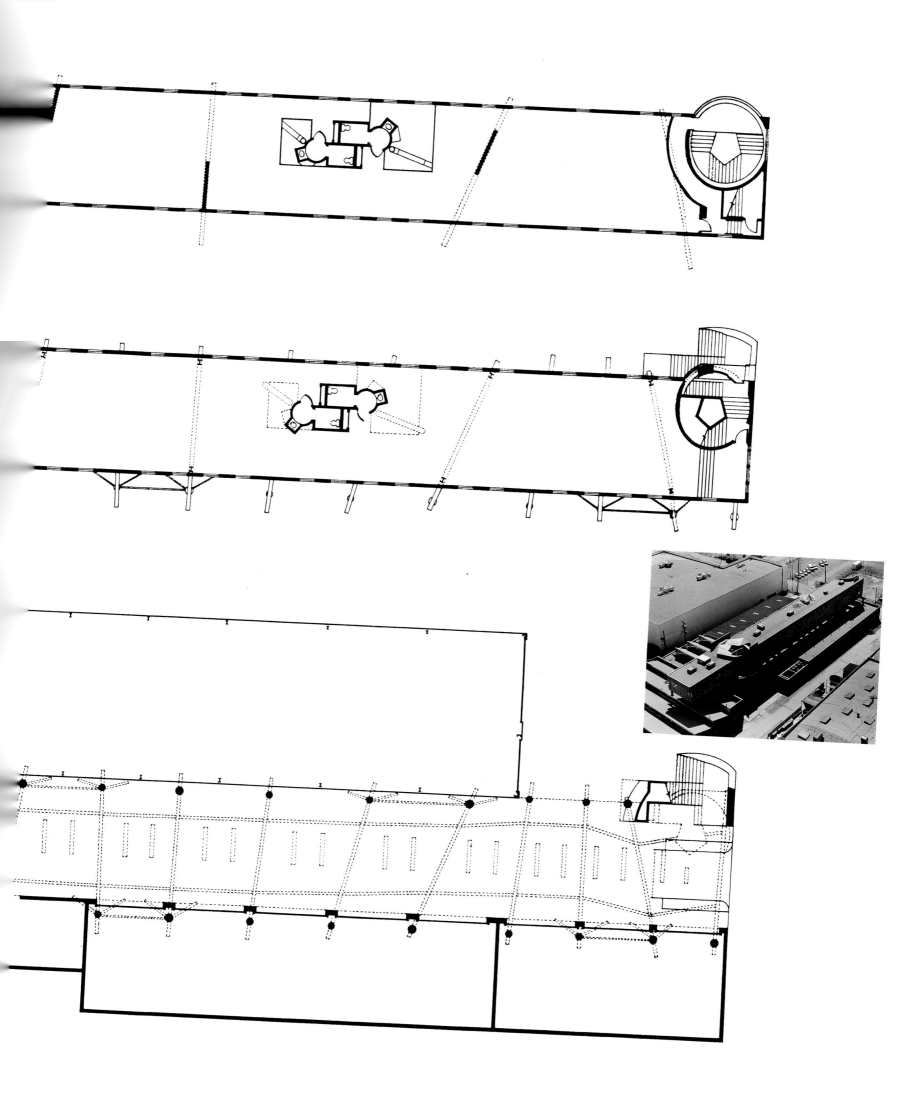

2.22

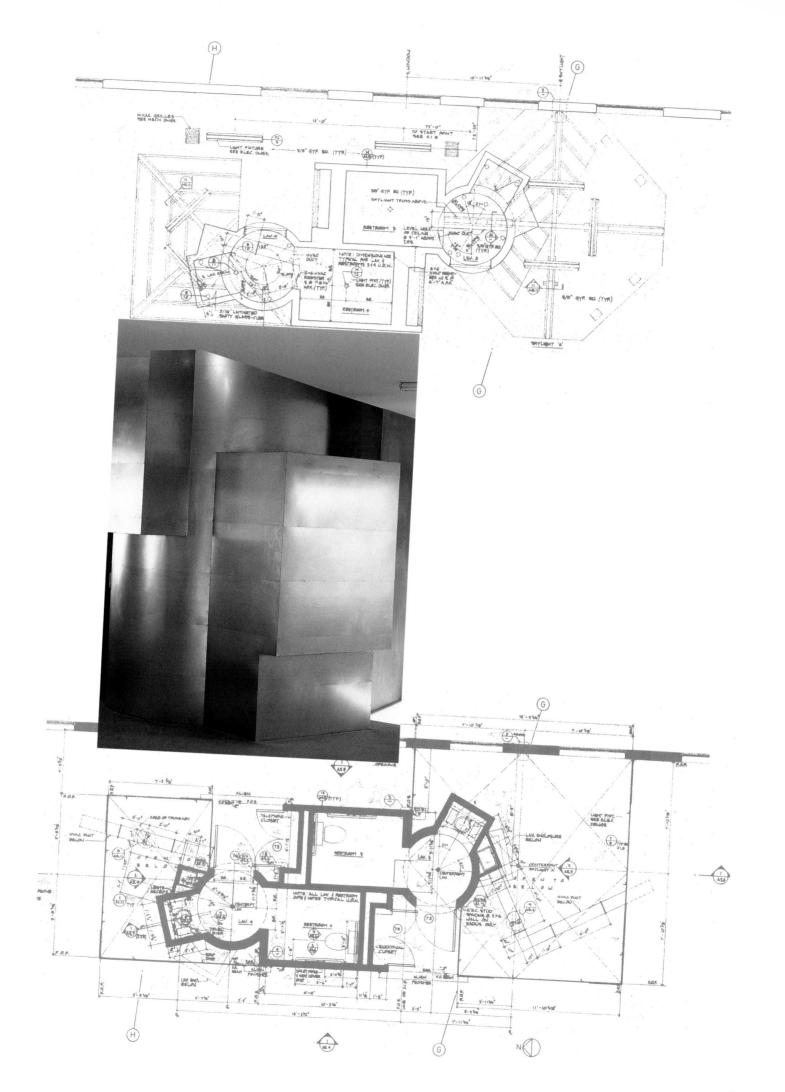

2.31

# 3
# THE GLUE

The glue is a cerebral underground from which specific conceptual undertakings are generated. The glue is a caricatured psyche. It designates a crisscross of emotions and ideas, piled up over many years, on which the architecture sits. The glue comes to bear in different ways, from different vantage points, at different weights, in various projects including the Samitaur project. But to say that you could actually find a particular image around a particular corner of Samitaur would be a misunderstanding. Start to disassemble the glue and it's gone. It's psychologically inviolate. Cut it into chunks to explain the mess and the interconnections are severed. The interconnections are so fine, so precarious, so infinitesimal, and so can't-be-numberedish, that it's not possible to break in. Nonetheless, the glue is an attempt to qualify that crisscross. There are concerns, aspirations, apprehensions, all running together in a kind of crazy flood. I couldn't sort it out clearly. And then all of a sudden something would pop up out of the web, and I could say, "Oh, there's a spider." And then the spider would be gone. It would be a misunderstanding to locate Chaplin or the Sistine Chapel or John Cage at Samitaur.

Over the years, as I continue to look and draw and travel and read, numerous disparate items have stuck in my head. Some enter and stay for a while. Some enter and transform. Some enter and go out the other side. What the composite is, I'm never quite sure—the list and the perspective keep moving.

## ABU SIM·BEL

The temples of Abu Simbel on the move, making way for the Aswan Dam, contradict the often repeated notion concerning the durability of buildings—that architecture endures. True; and utterly untrue.

We don't know what we've lost—at the bottom of the sea, under an avalanche, to floods and earthquakes. We guess. We surmise. We hypothesize. Perhaps whole cultures are lost. **Were Aeschyles, Sophocles, Aristophanes, and Euripides really the best, or are the best sitting on the bottom of the Aegean?** This shrine, this colossal Egyptian construction, was cut and moved so the Aswan waters couldn't swallow it. Where are all the pieces the waters swallowed? Abu Simbel had no site sanctity. How enduring is a site? Alter it. Manicure it. And in time become subject to being moved. Moving and being moved. Abu Simbel is majestic, maybe utterly beyond our ability to empathize and to re-create. We need these unknowable constructions across time that outrun time. Progress can't run in only one direction.

## AIR·PLANE

When my father died, I wondered why I was combing my hair, why I was doing anything given the inevitable conclusion. But something seemed mysteriously to push me. And keeps pushing me, even when it would be logical to stop. Sisyphus. Perhaps the push comes from a continuity force. Keep going, somehow, and invent a step in order to arrive at the next step, which requires the next invention. I agreed with myself to accept the possibility that I could formulate a plan, even though I couldn't say how long-term the plan was: a provisional paradigm.

Tatlin[1] makes Icarus real. The dream of flight. What's great about Tatlin's glider is its innocence and enthusiasm. No ideology, no method yet, just an instinct. The pre-idol machine, the machine before Chaplin[2] needed to stick his face in the gears. The machine as prospect, as experiment, not as certainty.

The technical events that first seem so astonishing have such short lives. The taller building, the longer bridge span, the faster plane doesn't appeal for long. **Technical wonders lose their wonder.** An ad for the movie *Airplane*. The wonder of flying isn't enough now to hold the attention of the audience. One has to twist the plane to entertain. This may account for some of the behavior in architecture today.

## AJAN·TA

Ajanta is one of these "I'm going to have to go there" places. Whether I get there or not, it's in my

1. See 3.30.
2. See 3.9.

head. Cave paintings of the Buddha from the second century BCE, eight hundred miles north and east of Bombay. A colossal number and, apparently, remarkable in quality. Difficult to photograph. Not much light. A transcendental sensibility that makes you enormously powerful while shedding the separation that makes you *you,* distinct from other yous. The art has an appeal because of its anonymity. The name of the artist is not important. But it is because it was left out, which tells you a lot about the intent of the religion. Ajanta might allow me to overcome Michelangelo's skull in the back wall of the Sistine Chapel.[3] It fascinates me and consoles me. There's a prospect. It's like the light coming under Kafka's Door of the Law.[4] You can see it. You might get to it, but you might not. This is an aspiration to a crucial experience in architecture. Tension. Maybe, maybe not. Architecture as contradictory prospects in the language of space.

AL·TA·MI·RA

The Altamira and Lascaux cave paintings, and recent discoveries at Chauvet and Cosquier, indicate how difficult it is to master our antecedents. What trails brought us to where we are? Contributors lost? Histories buried? We don't know whether tomorrow someone's submarine will bump into Atlantis, which might explain the perplexing continuities between forms, beliefs, and traditions in the Middle East and the Yucatán. Can we ever get to the bottom? To the ultimate explanation? **Why do we so consistently act as if we've arrived there, only to be forced to reverse our positions? What we don't know is always much bigger than what we do know.**

In the *Los Angeles Times* there was a story about the discovery of a skeleton in Spain, which, according to the author, entirely reexplains the chronology of human evolution. Now, says the story, we really know what happened. Evolution is no longer Darwin's hypothesis,[5] but more a process of fits and starts, successes and cul-de-sacs. The process of arriving at current humanity was described in the story as just as much a wonderful accident as a logical process.

The twenty-thousand-year-old head of the bull in the wall painting questions the current propensity to relegate to the antiquities file material from the 1960s or the 1980s because this, of course, is the up-to-date 1990s. The ultimate in sophistication, but the 1980s? How tedious and out-of-date. From this perspective almost everything that is hip is soon out of date. Then along comes Altamira with the most colossal and powerful art. These paintings are quite viable in their power and are durable and contemporary and relevant in every sense. The Madison Avenue notion that our tools and our songs will get better or more sophisticated over time, yet age so quickly, has to be evaluated in terms of the superficial currents of an ad-agency culture. Keep selling, keep the goods moving. Durability stifles sales (including art sales). **Deeper trends run on a different timeline.** Maybe there is just a string of good things outside time.

3. See 3.29.
4. See 3.24 (Progress).
5. See 5:8.

## AM·A·ZON

Amazon River Once Flowed West

"Amazon River Once Flowed West." And not only that. Perhaps the change in the direction of water flow from west to east was not Darwinian, not slow, not gentle, not gradual, not regular, not over eons. Perhaps it was instantaneous, like the asteroid hitting Jupiter[6]—cataclysmic instant change. How to bring that sensibility to architecture—Dionysus over Apollo[7]—**a sensibility that suggests the world moves by jumps and fits and huge digressions?** If science confirms geologically that the Amazon River once flowed west, we'll have to modify the logical, sequential perceptions of God the Geometer.[8]

## ANAT·O·MY LES·SON OF DR. TULP

Rembrandt—a corpse and a surgeon, explaining man to men. It all makes recognizable, empirical sense. One part of the anatomy is attached to another. **There is a sequence and a continuity and an order and a logic. This is in man,** and that empirical logic governs the entire cosmos—not just man, but man's world. So let's celebrate the mathematics of Pythagoras[9] and the logic of anatomy by placing man's grid on the moon.[10] Find the logic and extend the logic. **But is the logic intrinsic?** Probably not. The idea that the order of things is ultimately discoverable, that it's amenable to rational scrutiny, is perhaps the vantage point of our culture at the end of the twentieth century. But I detect substantial cracks in this viewpoint. **Is logic simply an imposed veneer over a subject that continues to throw it off?**

## ANG·KOR WAT

The civilization of Angkor Wat was at a pinnacle in the tenth, ninth, or eighth century BCE, before finally giving way to the trees. Architecture is so often talked about as durable. But it occurs to me that **the most durable form of architecture might be in print because, almost inevitably, tenants and clients and time all kick at buildings.** However powerful the building, however strong its ability to withstand the kicking, however successful the architect is in delivering a built experience that's powerful and human-controlled, the building is not able to withstand the forces that ultimately roll over (or is it through?) everything. **If you don't mow the lawn, it eats the street.**

In *The Lost World* there is a scene where lots of tiny dinosaurs overwhelm a man. He can whack away one, two, five, ten—but finally, he is unrecognizable. This happens to buildings. If you write a poem and the editor starts cutting words, punctuation, the title, you're left with fragments—like Gilgamesh. Or pieces of the Dead Sea Scrolls. We don't have the real Gilgamesh, too much is missing. You have to surmise. Intriguing, but not what the author intended. Angkor Wat? Maybe the people who inhabited these colossal buildings anticipated that someday

6. See 3.17.
7. See 3.11.
8. See 3.14.
9. See 3.25. See also 5:7.
10. See 3.20 (Moon Map).

someone would come and find not them or their progeny, but a tree growing where the king used to sit.

**The tree and the king experience pushes me.** I went to see *The Lost World* because I love looking at those animals. I've been like that since I was a little kid. I remember going to the Museum of Natural History in New York and looking at big skeletons of prehistoric whales. They were so powerful. What happened to all that power? Where does it go?

### BAB·Y·LON

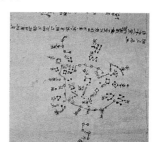

A very old drawing, a Babylonian map of the sky. It's consistent with culture's need to map. Umberto Eco's[11] Causaubin said, "Make a plan." **A plan seems to be a cultural essential necessary to account for the order of things.** If one can understand the order of things past, then presumably one can account for the present and predict the future. Very cogent.

The Babylonians had a map of the sky and, of course, it's incorrect. It leaves out lots of things. Ours does too. That's harder to take. But the tendency to continue to make maps or plans and to insist on the efficacy of those explanations seems consistent in every culture. From a distance we can see how those patterns or maps or plans have come and gone, although a suspicion of our own efforts doesn't always follow.

I recall being taught that we knew almost everything and just had to fill in a few of the details. **My sense now would be that we know almost nothing with certainty,** and that we can never know enough, have sufficient information to counter the inscrutable in our lives. Fundamentally, all these cultures, past and present, seem to want to say they know how the world works; who its villains are; how history moves, if it does, and who's going to move it—**Hegel to Marx**[12] **to Lenin**[13] **to Mao to Castro to oblivion. The Berlin Wall is down, or is it?** Makes the taking of definitive positions on history extremely tenuous, because you can see them disappear before your eyes. Somebody carts away the city in a truck,[14] a tree grows out of Angkor Wat's foundations.[15] Lenin sweeps out the trash, and then he himself is swept away.

### BACK UP THE TRUCK

A truck backing up and hauling away the American city. Presumably intent on making room to build the next one. The return of Marinetti and Futurist hygiene. It also seems particularly applicable to Los Angeles. Building there often seems so ephemeral. The conflict seems to be between erasing the city and remodeling it, retaining the city quite literally and restoring it, or the in-between, **recollecting forward**[16]**—retaining a residual aspect of the previous pattern and reincorporating it in a revised perception.** A lived, felt experience is sustained over time only by reevaluating priorities and reconstituting symbols. Redundancy stretched across

11. See 3.12 (Foucault's Pendulum).
12. See 5:10.
13. See 3.18.
14. See 3.5 (Back Up the Truck).
15. See 3.4. See also 3.7 (Buddha).
16. See 3.18 (Klee). See also 1.6, 1.11 and 5:9.

time exhausts the original vitality. What was once fresh becomes a tedious method, no longer an instinct, and the light goes out.

## BERKE·LEY

An antiwar gathering slide I shot in 1967 in Berkeley—the student movement against the Vietnam War and against the authority of the regents who were running the university. A great instructional process for me in human behavior. I had a chance to observe the effect of crowds on the individuals who made them up, what happened to individual identity as a consequence of the collective ethos of the crowd. The crowd as power. I started to consider social and political allegiances and the polarization of arguments, the caricature each side often delivers of the opposing position. The old Malcolm X line was quoted there a lot, and still is— you're either a part of the problem or a part of the solution. I had a feeling that **each person actually carries both the problem and the solution within themselves.** What I disliked in someone, I often found in myself. I could never line up with one side or the other because I could see each side cartooning its position in a way that excluded the other side, when, in fact, there was almost always some useful truth buried in the most onerous position. The strategic intent was always to crush the opposition. In many cases I just felt I was dancing in the middle.

The related issue has to do with defining the world as numbers, as masses, as gargantuan collective parts. There was a constant diatribe from the left and right: "the masses" need this and "the people" need that. **I wanted to understand life lived singly, one person at a time.** Life is personal and private, and not always exchangeable. Yacking about the interest of "the masses" would destroy life as it's lived, life by life. Each person has a story.

This leads to the question of whether generalizing about groups and group behavior is productive. This relates to the military theory debate: the West Point theory and the Sandhurst theory and the playing fields of Eton that produced all the famous British generals versus Tolstoy's idea that what war was really about was one man on one horse, falling in the mud, looking at the smoke, and having no sense of the general's a priori format, of how he fit in, that the cavalry was here and the infantry was there—a theory of masses, versus a single life. **The tension between the two sides of that argument is important to the Gnostic discussion. It's impossible to make circumstances intelligible in the world strictly by talking about groupings, numbers, or tendencies that obliterate the idiosyncrasies or the nuances of the individual.** Since I don't live my life collectively, that individuated, personal aspect has to be acknowledged. **The Gnostic argument has to do with the conception of knowledge arrived at in an internal, private, introverted way,** not something that is taken from a loudspeaker addressing a crowd of fifteen thousand people.

## BROOKS BROTH•ERS

A slightly disheveled character, Brooks Brothers–ish coat and tie, looking around to determine whether he wants to go with vitamins or shock or biofeedback or meditation. The confusion of life and **the difficulty of finding venues or avenues that make the less intelligible more intelligible.** You can find people, some motivated by kindness and convictions and some more mercantile, who will provide you the key to alleviating confusion. So they say. My experience is that there is no single key because there is no single lock. The problem may be deciding on an allegiance that, in many cases, vilifies other plausible alternatives.

There is an argument for not accepting everything in total but for accepting pieces of things, in different weights, at different times, and for continually reevaluating, adding and eliminating, **not necessarily with the idea that you would ever arrive at a conclusion that would be final** and that would explain everything. The personal paradigm could shift, and one would be willing to accept that. There's a quote by Reinhold Niebuhr, a remarkable religious thinker in the middle years of the twentieth century who said something that is now on every subway wall. Everybody knows it; whether anybody can put it into effect is a different matter. Niebuhr's remarks have to do with the need to have the courage to understand and change what can be understood and changed, to let go what can't be, and to know the difference between the two prospects. There's a line from Kant: "From the crooked timber of humanity no straight thing could ever be made." **But crooked, if it were a path for living, would be the only straight path.**

## BUD•DHA

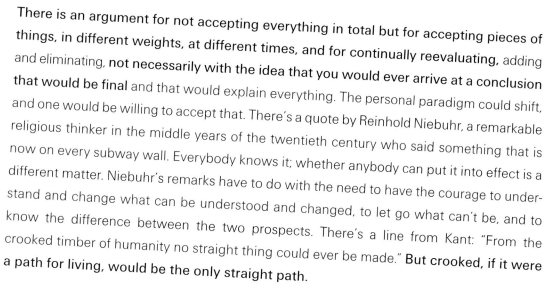

This overgrown Buddha shares qualities with the tree growing out of the roof of Angkor Wat.[17] Buddha admonished us not to build statues, images of him. Someone, apparently, wasn't listening. The statue was built, as it often is, contrary to the recommendation, and time is devouring the result (no Buddhist surprise). Siddhartha Gautama surely appreciated the force that seems to be continually producing and devouring as the planet metamorphoses. Something keeps pushing up, pushing up the new, turning over, devouring the old. That sense of time moving is an aspect of Gnostic architecture. Put another way, architecture should include the spirit of the Buddha devoured by the forest.

## CAGE

Whatever John Cage was taught about writing music was apparently inadequate to express his interests. Therefore he had to amend the form. What he did was to make decisions about what he heard based on what he saw. It's a graphic association of notes connecting points with

17. See 3.4.

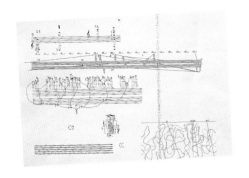

lines and points with other points visually, so that the visual aesthetic of the music has a substantial role in determining what the auditory aesthetic is. And the ear takes the consequences. Cage is asking what music is. Is it what is written, what is played, what we hear, what is heard and remembered, or what one sees?

## CAR·A·COL I

A Mayan building in Chichen Itzá almost foreign to its urban context, since all the other city's buildings have consistent plans and sections. The only building discovered thus far in the Yucatán that has a roof dome, a circular plan, and a helical section. The section is quite complicated—helix and dome together. We might call the Caracol an observatory. But it was as much a religious structure. Its purpose seems to have been to discover the mysteries of the skies, to map the skies, and to communicate that pattern, that predictable pattern, to the local population. **A unique building with a unique purpose that we probably can't account for in the terms that made it intelligible to the Mayans. So we try to define it in terms we recognize.**

The exegesis by the local docents is that the building was designed to track the behavior of Venus as an object in the sky, but the extraordinary power, the physicality of the building and the relative weakness of Venus in the sky don't seem to square. The building is also apparently related to a fifty-two-year celestial cycle. There is a theory (however wild) that Venus, according to both Indo-European and Middle Eastern myths, was born out of the head of Jupiter, rocketing around the sky, possibly as a comet, for a period of time and threatening the earth. I don't know how plausible that idea is scientifically, although the force of the building seems to warrant such a unique and powerful explanation—like a culture facing imminent disaster. A purely cerebral conception of astronomy is ours, not theirs.

## CA·RA·COL II

Detail of the dome of the Caracol, the Venusian religious observatory in the Yucatán. An absolutely unique configuration in a society that developed systematic wall and section configurations that were applied to a variety of building types—almost a standardized building system. And then comes this unprecedented anomaly with its astro-religious purpose, housing the observers who watched the sky so that the society could be informed and protected. A unique building type, a unique purpose, intentionally antithetical to the surrounding typology. **The purposeful contradiction of antecedents has a long civic pedigree. Breaking tradition is also a long tradition.**

From Mumford's *The Myth of the Machine.*[18] Here is the overwhelmed/overwhelming modern city and the cemetery juxtaposed. The question is whether the life-form of the modern city points inexorably to death. Is there a city of life or only the city of death? Is the ubiquitous machine the driver and the local citizenry simply a homogenized passenger in the contemporary city? The machine's city? Can the city sustain what is private and personal and inventive for its inhabitants, one life at a time? Is the mass man, the machine-conscripted man, the urban man we know?

Chaplin on the wheel, memories of Berkeley[19] in 1967, with Mario Savio hyperbolizing in Sproul Plaza: how to throw your body on the gears of the odious academic machine. Chaplin reflects on the primacy of the human who once made the machine and is now dwarfed by it, in awe of what he created, a machine that is liable to run away with him. Should he run with the machine? In contemporary architecture the machine and gears have become, in the hands of some, an idol. **The machine aesthetic, as an allegiance, ignores the fragile sensibility it had when it first tentatively arose** in the hands of Jean Prouvé[20] and Marcel Lods early in the twentieth century—science and its technical progeny tied to a belief in progress—heat the houses, light the streets, zip around in automobiles. What was difficult has become easy, and everybody is happier as a consequence (so they reasoned).

Change and progress were conceived explicitly in opposition to an earlier perception of order, constancy, and stability. There was a new clientele. Previously the aristocracy, the monarch, the church were the clients. Now it is the people and the analogue machine making the happy democratic city for the masses as first-time clients. The machine is no longer a respondent but an end in itself, Chaplin intervenes to contest the primacy of the depersonalized, institutionalized, bureaucratic machine. I can't talk about "the masses."

**Gnostic architecture has to do with a perception, that one by one, one can amend the perception of what's real,** so one is not run over or devoured by the real or metaphysical machine. This critique doesn't deify the antithesis of the machine either. It's not a way of saying machines aren't productive or able to make some things better sometimes. It's the machine as conceptually neutral. **The machine is what we say it is, not what it says we are.**

The first image is the snake-head end of an impossible-to-climb stair up the face of the pyramid. The second image is of a podium where sacrifices were made in the Chacmol. The two are

18. See 3.20.
19. See 3.6.
20. See 5.6.

physically close and open to the sky. The sky is their roof.

I remember going to see an exhibition in Los Angeles on the Mayans. The exhibit characterized the Mayans as the Greeks of the New World. The exhibit makers assumed that cultural credence in the Yucatán was certified by associating the Indian culture with a pedigreed Western antecedent.

My experience wandering through the Yucatán, marveling at the power of its building, was not so different from my visit to Stonehenge. In both cases I felt a driving, pre-cerebral force, generally foreign to the West. Mayan architecture challenges the fragile, tenuous circumstances of living with a survivor's paradigm. What an astonishing responsibility for architecture to carry. That confidence is contagious. It wills a culture forward. But not ours. We're immersed in our own contradictions, lacking the impetus to a transcendent will. For the Mayans, calculation, analysis, and method are subordinated to the power of a cogent worldview. For us, those means only ratify our piecemeal predilections.

## THE CON·SCI·ENCE OF WORDS

One shall seek nothingness only to find a way out of it and one shall mark the road for everyone.

This could be a Gnostic paradigm. It's a statement of the moral imperative driving Canetti's intellect and his art. That is, **one might wander into nihilism looking for ways to formulate a pattern, a ladder, a road, a rope out**—now I'm thinking of the rope quote "Two feet lower and a halo becomes a noose." In Canetti's terms **the poet's task is to take an inherited conceptual model apart and leave a record of the disassembled or reassembled pieces so that others who come later to the same ground can find support in those efforts.** That wouldn't necessarily mean that the next poet would go further or that there was really a "further" to go. Rather each new attempt at understanding might proceed to the same place but by a different route. The poet's moral imperative is to "make the road" for whoever else wants to make it.

## COUR·AGE

I have the courage, I believe, to doubt everything; I have the courage, I believe, to fight with everything; but I have not the courage to know anything; not the courage to possess, to own anything.

A statement of self-confidence from Søren Kierkegaard. A statement of humility. **To make a building I have to own a paradigm temporarily. By owning I mean conceptualizing an allegiance or hypothesis as space. But while it's constructed it's simultaneously contested,** put up, pulled down, like Penelope's weaving—together and apart. Assembly includes disassembly. But the object is not to return to zero. **The object is not to claim permanent residence. This is a transient's paradigm.**

## CRE·A·TION IS AN OUT-PA·TIENT SEARCH

The original sketch comes from Le Corbusier. It advocates a balance, half a head of Apollo on the left, half a head of Dionysus on the right—bilaterally symmetrical. The Apollonian aspect is cerebral, rational. The Dionysian aspect represents spirit and psyche—the soul.[21] Measured and unmeasured again.

I rotated the drawing ninety degrees so the figure of **Dionysus is a vast underpinning,** and reduced Apollo with the photocopier, so **the rational aspect is a tiny speck floating in that huge Dionysian sea.** The intention is to communicate that **rationality is an anomaly in something much bigger.** Dionysus and Apollo no longer equals, no longer symmetrical; Apollo the exception, Dionysus the dominant rule.

## DE·GAS

*Ballerinas.* **The painting suggests the possibility of alternative kinds of balance.** There is the balance of standing firmly—a durable balance. Then there is the fragile, delicate balance—one that clearly won't be sustained. For the ballerina, the more tenuous the balance, the more artistic the performance. And we already know the limits of that precarious position. We know the conclusion at the beginning. It doesn't have a long life, but it has a power because of the delicacy and the lack of durability. I think that poignancy, created by **the tension between the time of implementation and the instant of collapse,** is very clearly a concern. **Gnostic architecture should communicate, in the language of its spaces, the ballerina's dialectic.**

## DI·O·NY·S·US AND APOL·LO

Commentary from Friedrich Nietzsche, in *The Birth of Tragedy.* The polemical poles, Dionysus and Apollo or, by a crude extrapolation, eros and intellect, cerebral and emotional, art and science—perhaps even yin and yang. So when the film viewer is with Kurosawa alone at the top of the mountain in *Ran,*[22] or with Brueghel staring bewildered at the *Triumph of Death,*[23] or following Canetti[24] in and out of nothingness, or trembling with Michelangelo on the back wall of the Sistine Chapel,[25] or misunderstanding with Kierkegaard[26] who laughs at his tears and cries at his laughter, art (in the most ecumenical sense) arrives with a very particular mission: to assuage a debilitated, diminished human capacity to go on. As T. S. Eliot wrote in *The Four Quartets* (quoting Krishna): "Not fare well, but fare forward voyagers."[27]

Here, when the danger to his will is greatest, art approaches as a saving sorceress, expert at healing. She alone knows how to turn these nauseous thoughts about the horror or absurdity of existence into notions with which one can live.

## FACE

An almost blank, almost featureless face. Unless you're an expert, it's difficult to tell whether the

21. See 3.11.
22. See 3.26. See also 5:11.
23. See 3.32.
24. See 3.10 (Conscience of Words).

25. See 3.29.
26. See 3.17.
27. See 5:3.

statue is quite old, or relatively contemporary. I use the statue as a **metaphor for conceptual strategizing in architecture.** If life is a blank face, one has to make the face or assign the face certain features in order to proceed, in order to say what life is. If there's no intrinsic face, then assigning features is not only problematic but you have to wonder about the longevity of the features that you assign. So the metaphor becomes one of acknowledging the responsibility for the features of the face, and anticipating that the features would change, so that **the paradigm is not a fixed paradigm** but an evolving or developing or shifting paradigm. Sometimes subtly, sometimes radically. I used to say that life was a blank face, but it's never entirely blank. There is always at least some residual recollecting of a previous assigning of features. To assign features, you have to erase the preceding features. As a more general pattern of behavior, **in order to do something I have to move something that preceded me out of the way.**

## THE FALL OF IC·A·RUS

The Brueghel painting *Landscape with the Fall of Icarus.* The dream of flight: Icarus with his sun-melted wax wings falling into the sea, and everyone else paying no attention. He falls, he drowns, the farmer continues to plow his field, perhaps afraid to look. Each life is its own subject. **Special efforts sometimes disappear.**

## FOU·CAULT'S PEN·DU·LUM

Randomly they throw in manuscript pages on hermetic thought. The Masters of the World, who live beneath the earth. The Comte de Saint-Germain, who lives forever. The secrets of the solar system contained in the measurements of the Great Pyramid. The Satanic initiation rites of the Knights of the Temple. Assassins, Rosicrucians, Brazilian voodoo. They feed all this into their computer, which is named Abulafia (Abu for short), after the medieval Jewish cabalist.

This is a quote taken from the jacket of Umberto Eco's *Foucault's Pendulum,* which may indicate someone thought this snippet was compelling advertising. It makes available, in an abbreviated way, qualities I find essential in defining the contemporary philosophical/historical condition, the intellectual environment that prevails at the moment. There is an enormous amount of empirical information available to us now, more than ever—anthropological, archaeological, historic, scientific, from diverse places and diverse times: Brazilian voodoo, the Comte de Saint-Germain, Rosicrucians, Crusaders. Every place, any time. We know about each of these subjects. We know of them as parts without a whole. So the proposed solution here (which is of course not really the solution) is to jam it all into the cabalistic computer, which will magically make it all cohere. **We have information we've never had, but we don't have any idea how to assemble the pieces, how to value one part relative to another, how to prioritize.** History as an unreconstructed mosaic of pieces that don't currently fit, but might later on. The theme of possible fit is very much the focus of Eco's novel. For Eco **there's an incredibly complicated, delicate, poignant, precarious, almost but not quite decipherable connecting tissue or sinew or web that might just possibly unite all the pieces.** Might. We can't detect it today; but tomorrow could be different. **The fact of parts and the aspiration to coherence,** that the pieces might confirm continuity as well as the more readily felt discontinuity: **that tension between possibilities is where Gnostic architecture begins.**

FUL·LER

Dome over midtown. That has an appeal, if only a perverse appeal. It also has an enormous confidence, an innocent's confidence. This would be the wheel without Chaplin[28] on it— the machine that lights the streets, heats the houses, and zips the populace around in cars— making the world better. The world moves forward as a consequence of our ability to apply technology, and deification was soon to follow. A colossal constructed space where people are understood as number, not nuance. **As Philip Johnson once said, "Don't try to put a door in a Buckminster Fuller dome." There's no room for personal entry and exit in that technological vision.**

GE·OL·O·GY I

A vast piece of geology. What it shows are eons of change, sometimes wild jumps that radically altered the history of the earth's surface, rips and tears that suggest a more cataclysmic theory of evolution. If I were to argue that architecture has to read and redirect such geologic revisionism, then this sense of the world moving by jumps, not according to a single, logical, synchronized system, should find its way into architecture. **It's plausible to argue that architecture** should not deal with painful subjects, that its job **ought to be to add solace and comfort and stability, and put its occupants at ease. That might be part of the job, part of the time; but if that were all of the job all of the time, architecture would divorce itself from subject matter that might lead the culture somewhere else.** Architecture would be reactionary, not progressive. A place to hide, as opposed to seek. **Architecture is not a place to hide.**

GE·OL·O·GY II

A cliff and a spectacular cliff dwelling. Human beings clinging to the layers of geology accumulated over eons. People picking holes in rocks. One could imagine some huge storm that would wash all human traces away. But the precariousness of the rock habitation, the fragility of it, is its beauty as well as its tension. I was thinking about the "preserve the environ- ment" subject, protecting the environment instead of digging into it. The sense that the earth has to be treasured is coming back again after a long time. **The first time around, in very prim- itive civilizations, the earth overwhelmed its peoples.** The wind blew you away, the snow froze you, the flood washed you out, and the animals ate you or chased you up trees. It was all too much. **The war between humanity and the environment has been a long one, arriving at the point, psychologically, where you could plow the snow, put the animals in the zoo, and put the flood in some concrete channel.** There are, of course, cracks in the concrete. But in general, it's possible to make a life absent of those apprehensions of nature. **We feel like masters of everything,** and now comes the concern that we've pushed too far and lost that awe of nature. So we look for a way to retrieve it. It's hard to do that without recognizing that the environment itself, however you characterize it, not only washed its inhabitants away for millennia but breaks itself up and remakes itself in perpetuity—the asteroid collision on Jupiter,[29] for instance. **It's not only human beings that disrupt the environment but the environment, in a cataclysmic way sometimes, that disrupts and destroys itself. Why is one of those acceptable, even welcome, and the other one intolerable?**

## GOD

**God isn't dead, survey shows**

Chicago Tribune

CHICAGO — A survey of 13 predominantly Judeo-Christian countries shows substantial majorities in most of them believe in God and in life after death, refuting perceptions of social scientists that society isn't as religious as it used to be.

"It is too early to write an obituary for religion," said Rev. Andrew [...] and a coordinator of the study Monday by the International [...] Program, "God die[...]

gious belief, the survey found that a majority of Christians and Jews reject church teaching on premarital sex.

The International Social Survey Program, a consortium of social science research centers, released its findings at its annual meeting convened Monday in Chicago. They are based on random surveys of 19,000 people, with a minimum of 1,000 in each of 13 countries, in 1991.

Among the survey's findings:
• Majorities in nine countries believe in life after death. Belief ranged from 80 percent in Ireland and 78 percent [...]

The local gentry was polled to determine the existence of a deity. Another case where statistical numerology may have nothing to do with the answer, where the answer may be precluded because of the way the question was posed. **I think the next question is not whether God is dead, but whether man is dead.** At least in terms of man's ability to come to some kind of terms with a conception of God that a pollster couldn't unravel.

## GOD THE GE·OM·E·TER

This medieval drawing is **an instance of a culture exteriorizing itself and calling the result God.** The culture's priorities become God's priorities. This could also be identified as a medieval prayer for order. So this is how the world was made, is made, will be made—with a compass, geometry, number, and logic, organized in an analytical way. The world is created using Euclid's[30] tools. So if one knows Euclid, one can provide an exegesis for the design of the cosmos, including the deity. Order can make life plausible, if God behaves as he's represented, and if you subscribe to this depiction. Of course, there is always the apprehension that God won't behave this way at all. When that apprehension is sufficiently strong, along comes the next deity.

## HAP·PY DAYS

The values of a suburban lifestyle. Gods provided. Culture homogenized. **An orderly, well-behaved, and predictable road map for living.** But happy isn't always happy. And what's happy architecture? Not to invent? Not to investigate? Not to speculate?

29. See 3.17.

30. See 3.27 (Rothko). See also 3.28 (School of Athens) and 5.2.

HEL·MET

Henry Moore's *Helmet,* an exegesis of which explains the structure of this book. A conventional helmet is a protective surround. The exterior form conforms to what it encloses. The two objects—the inside (head: eyes, ears, nose, mouth) and the outside (helmet)—are essentially congruent; the inside of one confirms the outside of the other. Henry Moore's version is somewhat more complicated. There is an external object sufficiently perforated with facelike holes that one can see that it encloses or surrounds or protects something else. But the interior shielded shape isn't coincident with the outer, as is the case with the traditional helmet. It is separated from the exterior and distinct in configuration. The inside shape is wrapped by the external form but the two are separated and different.

As with this book, **there's the outside of the outside form, the inside of the outside form, and then a space in perpetual tension. Then there's the outside of the inside form and, finally, the inside of the inside form.** The sculpture could serve as a psychological model for perpetual unraveling, in the sense that one could continue to go further and further in. More pieces, more spaces, more tension. So the model can be understood as either finite or infinite. *Helmet* is also an aesthetic amalgam for the relationships between shapes. **Outside and inside are both coincidental and discontinuous. Fit and misfit.**

HY·BRID MON·STER

This creature stands with many companions along a funeral road near Beijing. On the way to death and on the way from death. **Why so many monsters,**[31] **one culture after another?** Are they psychologically real? Do they reflect the psychological deficiencies of a culture's attempt to represent a logical world order? Could the monster stand for what we don't know, can't reach, but can at least vaguely imagine? Can architecture include the "can't know" or the "dimly known"?

I·SE SHRINE

This is the Taoist shrine at Ise near Kyoto, originally constructed during the seventh century CE. The shrine and its related subject matter were introduced to me by Kenzo Tange, with whom I studied in 1971. The shrine posits two sites, one temporarily vacant and one where a temple is temporarily constructed. The built temple stands for twenty years. After twenty years, it is demolished and rebuilt in the identical way, with new materials, on the adjacent site. This process continues in perpetuity. So **the building is fixed, constant, unmoving, and eternal, and at the same time it is in flux, ephemeral, changing, and limited.** Ise is both **in time and**

31. See 3.18 (Lurking Monster).

out of time, literally embodied. I once gave a lecture where I used Ise as the principal image. It was entitled "the square with no corners," from a quotation by the Taoist philosopher Lao Tzu. The Ise shrine is an effort to build physically what "the square with no corners" suggests conceptually. It is quite simple to have no corners, and it might not be difficult to have a square, but the square with no corners is an insurmountable assignment for the Western God the Geometer.[32] And it confirms the problematic nature of the effort to transfer the language of philosophy to the language of space.

## JAI·PUR

A detail from the public plaza in Jaipur. This Moghul construction belongs to the eighteenth century. There is a series of these sky-measuring devices on an enormous public plaza, informing the public about the precise relationship between earth, planets, and stars. Time and the movement of the earth become part of the observable order and part of the built mechanism—astronomy for the citizens to climb on as well as for the scientists. **The tools for this public presentation of astronomy are tactile and tangible and colossal in scale—stone and concrete—as well as abstract and cerebral.**

When I proposed the Vesey Street project for Battery Park in New York, a publicly accessible cosmology was integral to the project. The Samitaur building uses an antecedent hourglass as a metaphor for the form of the entry stair. The grains of sand might be the people moving up and down the stairway. So it is a time-reversing hourglass. Time moves backward and forward here as the inhabitants move up and down. **The question of time and cosmology needn't be so solemn.** I have an interest in finding a way to bring that subject matter, happy and sad, to architecture: humanity as party to the earth and sky, and humanity disowned by the same parties. Around and around and around.

## JOYCE

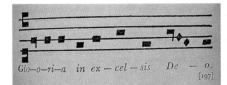

Glo—o—ri—a  in  ex — cel — sis  De  —  o.
[197]

The literary application of a musical score in James Joyce's *Ulysses:* **the dissolution of conventional literary boundaries,** a visual as opposed to an auditory role for music notation. The musical staff and score become literature. The traditional compositional rules are gone—no requisite capital letter, noun, verb, or period as obligatory sentence structure. No longer is music to be understood as simply listening. That a phonetic or notational language—a form, a way of understanding and communicating—is taught or learned, inherited or internalized by students, does not mean the language is intrinsically the language. That form of language communication is generic and extrinsic when it's inherited. It becomes specific and intrinsic to its user as it becomes personalized.

32. See 3.14.

Joyce took Homer's 2,800-year-old story and remodeled it. He moved the document to a different time zone, not necessarily by erasing it all but by using Homer as a frame of reference to be laboriously elaborated.

This score for God, as part of Joyce's text, is not only intellectual, it's visual, like e. e. cummings stringing letters and words all over the page. But the line between music and literature has stretched and blurred to encompass new conceptual options. Therefore, the question of what music is or what literature is or what, by implication, architecture is, is open. There is no dependable dictionary for those who are inclined to redefine a door, a wall, a roof, a window, a space.

## JU·PI·TER

A recent photograph from *Time* magazine of Jupiter devastated, struck by an enormous asteroid. Whose sky calendar predicted that event? If I extrapolate from the asteroid strike to the legend of Venus tracked by the priests of the Caracol[33] I could arrive at an intrinsically unstable world or unstable worldview, as opposed to predictable, measurable behavior of the planets and stars. The subject is similar to the story in the *New York Times* suggesting that the Amazon River[34] used to flow in the opposite direction and perhaps reversed direction in an instant. I don't know if any of this is so, but it has a plausible logic for me. The belief that cosmological change could occur in a moment, rather than imperceptibly over millennia, might again be man's making himself comfortable, inventing a pro forma by which his needs can be measured—sequential, logical, step-by-step. Using such a method, we can decipher and predict, we can anticipate, as opposed to—uh oh, here comes the asteroid. A different, unpredictable evolution is conceived as discontinuous leaps, not regular, systematic steps: asteroids on Jupiter, not Darwin on Earth.[35]

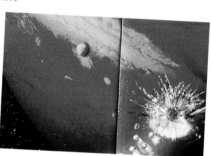

## KIER·KE·GAARD

Kierkegaard was the author who admonished his readers not to quote him at all—not to break the seamless fabric of his text—so this quotation defies that admonition. Does it follow that no real understanding is ever possible? Or does it follow that if one dismantles one's own misunderstandings a true understanding can be arrived at? Suppose we really have everything backward or upside down? An understanding, a stance seems to be necessary to proceeding in the world, and yet our ordering ideas seem consistently inadequate. What if up were really down, or right were really wrong? Kierkegaard also said "So also what I write contains the notice that everything is to be understood in such a way that it is revoked, that the book has not only an end but a revocation." So understanding is and isn't. I sometimes feel the self-confidence, the energy, the prospect of saying "this is the way it is," knowing no source outside

What if everything in the world were a misunderstanding, what if laughter were really tears?

33. See 3.8.
34. See 3.4.
35. See 3.3 (Altamira). See also 5:8.

the self, succeeds. I don't think this is arrogance, although it might be misread as if it were, because simultaneously I feel I can't succeed, can't possibly comprehend, and it's useless to try. This is neither cynical nor negative nor nihilistic—none of those. It's simply that the mystery is utterly beyond our ability to penetrate it intellectually.

What I've proposed, in architectural terms—the dialectical lyric—is an intentional oxymoron. The dialectic suggests the intellectual tension in Kierkegaard's quote, but the lyric would allow a transcendent experience beyond this contradiction. That doesn't eliminate the dialectic in an intellectual way, but it might allow one to overcome it in a spiritual way. **This is architecture as religion in the most ecumenical sense, which is Gnostic architecture's first sense.**

## KLEE

This painting by Paul Klee is actually a city-planning subject, perhaps unintended by the artist. It can be understood as a representation of how the city reflects itself, extends itself, reengenders itself. How does the modern city enlarge, extend, replace its pieces, reinvent or rediscover what it is or what it could be? The city can't extend itself by mirroring its history in a narcissistic manner. The city can't fall so deeply in love with its reflected image that it drowns in its own redundancy. **We have to find a way of acknowledging the essential residual consequences of yesterday in order to push or to move the definition of the city beyond its memory.** This is recollecting forward,[36] which is precluded by simply memorializing yesterday.

## LE·NIN

This constructivist poster, Lenin sweeping out the predictable villains—bankers, monarchs, priests; *The Threepenny Opera*'s diabolical characters—is not unrelated to the Prince of Wales's[37] discussion. The association between political allegiances and aesthetic vantage points is rare in the United States but strong in Europe. I'm not for those easy associations, but I am for the sense that architecture's space isn't only aesthetic. Politics—the machinations of human relationships—isn't deep enough either, or personal enough; you have to be private before being public. A cast of angelic characters and villains won't do it, which is not to say that the politics of the architect are the politics of his or her work. The two might be quite different from one another, regardless of what the architect claims.

## LURK·ING MON·STER

A neurosis? Counting the boards on the fence is a little like counting the cracks in the sidewalk. Who is the lurking monster? Will numerology make it disappear? Who is the apprehensive counter?

36. See 3.5 (Back Up the Truck). See also 1.6, 1.11, and 5:9.
37. See 3.24. See also 3.29 (Sistine Chapel).

3.18

Do monsters appear only in the cracks or should monsters be counted along with the planks? Is the monster part of the order or out of order? **Is what's required a way of conceptualizing architecture that includes its demons?** Does that mean inventing space that incorporates these antipathies? **Perhaps the monster was simply imagined.**

MA·CHU PIC·CHU

This perhaps instigated the early images of Samitaur and those regularly irregular, almost orthogonal blocks that had to be tamed and strapped together. That original piecemeal building concept was bundled and tied together. Otherwise the whole assembly would have burst apart. Like Patfard Clay's student union,[38] it seems audacious, but in a different way from Clay's San Francisco State project. Its enormous walls and huge stones (and the colossal effort needed to move those stones) represent inexorable power. It had to be there; it had to be done. But this is a societal effort, a cultural decision, by what slaves or free people, by what priestly or monarchical admonitions I don't know. The audacity is collective, as opposed to the San Francisco State student union, which is more private, more precarious, in a time when there is no collective audacity. **There is a collective skittishness and conservatism—better weigh it, better measure it, better analyze it, and, in the end, like J. Alfred Prufrock, it's a life** measured out with coffee spoons.

THE MAD·MAN

Years ago I used this painting by Courbet as an introduction to a lecture. I remember saying "Architecture is the act of a desperate man." That sounds a little melodramatic. **I don't think I was quite prepared to say that architecture was the act of a madman.** This discussion reminds me of a remark by Gilbert Chesterton, a British ironist, who claimed that "the madman is the man who has lost everything but his reason." **I used this subject matter to suggest that architecture is generated from a precarious psychological state, existing in a dialectical tension,** without any paradigmatic allegiance. The need was to sustain a number of contradictory (maddening?) possibilities simultaneously. I could never become the man who arrives at an intersection where there are multiple roads leading in and out and insists that there is only one way to proceed. The option to go down several roads at once and, if required, come back to the origin must be sustained. **Continuing along a single road so that ultimately the other roads become roads that never were is not an option that interests me.** The architect documents his or her own journey. The prospect of going down all roads is inconceivable—who could know them all? But I want the work to indicate a consciousness that these other possibilities remain alive.

## MOON MAP

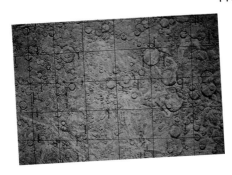

A contemporary photographic map of the moon, courtesy of Caltech or MIT—an indication of a certain way of understanding. Our way. Our time. It's a map of a portion of the moon with a grid superimposed, based on the assumption that the Cartesianizing of the surface is synonymous with the development of an understanding of that surface. To grid something, to geometricize a surface, is to begin to comprehend according to this premise. The grid does give a measurable legibility, but is legibility, numbers and dimensions, synonymous with understanding? **The moon doesn't give a damn about our grid. The grid has more to say about the people who are imposing it, who claim it's a way of objectifying what's external to them. But it's only a way of subjectively interpreting how we define what is objective. I** could say measuring objectifies. But I think the idea of measuring leaves out the important immeasurables.

I did a lecture that, borrowing from Kafka's diaries, I called "Coughing Up the Moon." That was Kafka's metaphor for his creative process.[39] The moon grid is anathema to the coughing-up-the-moon metaphor. **Kafka's image is beyond the reach of the grid.** In fact, the more moon you grid, the less moon you can cough up. I don't know whether the two sensibilities could run together. To be conscious of both is to know the insufficiency of either. But for the moment this is simply a point about the limits of the grid-mind and the subjectivity of what is claimed to be objective, subjectivity not necessarily being a pejorative term.

## MUM·FORD

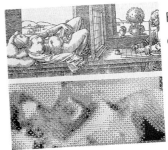

From *The Myth of the Machine:* how we see and what we see and whether what we see, or what we hear for that matter, is what somebody else sees, either from across the room or across the centuries. The first image has to do with the development of an empirical drawing technique, linear perspective, which makes scientific the perspectival reproduction of the eye. The truth as an abstraction. The second image, computerized, follows logically. The human digitized, no longer the truth as individual, as particular. Is it one life at a time, or is it one generic life? The larger, the noisier the culture becomes, the more difficult it is to depict the questions of living, one life at a time.

## MUS·TANG II BORE·DOM O

**Mustang II. Boredom O.** Here's an old automobile advertisement that is probably self-explanatory. The proposition is that the problems of today's short attention spans can be resolved by the continual purchasing of novelties—life experience as commodity. You have to buy the next one and the next one and the next one. The ultimate solution is never a prospect because that would mean you could stop buying. **That's a culture with an outside but no inside,** culture determined externally, which

39. See 3.24 (Progress).

suggests an interior void. **Not uncoincidentally, our most powerful built symbols, high-rise buildings, are like that. The image, the power, is an extroverted manifestation of potency, not the nine-foot floor-to-ceiling heights into which the occupants are stuffed.** Madison Avenue sells buildings, like it sells Mustangs, with outsides and no insides.

## NAZ•CA

The plains of Nazca is a very large desert in the Peruvian highlands. The lines are deep cuts in the stone surface of the desert, colossal etchings of animal figures that can't be read clearly from the ground but are legible from the sky. The drawings are presumably addressed to a natural force or to a deity who could understand or read from on high. I would liken the drawings to the conception of God the Geometer.[40]

Here's a long-disappeared culture that begins in the most elementary way to order itself, to organize its life, to establish value, to make gods, and, therefore, starts to conceive a world that is ordered and organized according to a particular strategy. God the Geometer tells us that God works with geometric precision, with analytical tools, so that life has a method that can be read using those tools. Likewise, the Nazca culture teaches itself what the primary qualities of living are, what issues are to be addressed, and in what form. The institutions and their physical symbols are established, etched in the culture physically and psychologically. Values are insisted upon. It's an aspiration for permanence. The culture first invents itself, then looks to its models to understand what to do. Like the face with no features,[41] Nazca is a prayer for order. **Nazca invents Nazca, then goes to Nazca and asks Nazca what Nazca should do.** There's something psychologically intriguing about that step. A little disingenuous? First you invent out of your experience, you give forms, give order, provide symbols and rules. Then you ask the rules you made what the rules are. In the end you're always asking yourself. Once you feel that, you get suspicious of following anybody else's method.

## OLD STONES

I remember a conductor, years ago, on the train to Salisbury Plain—he said, "Are you going to see the Old Stones?" You can't get there today. Now there's a fence around the Old Stones. Maybe Stonehenge isn't new or old. Perhaps age is not its subject. There's a power and confidence here. It's instinct, culture as instinct first. (Method soon follows.) Which doesn't mean it has no cerebral organizational component. Here intellect is the arbiter of an inventive instinct to force a new force out of that barren landscape. **Contemporary cosmology comes out of the barrel of nearsighted telescopes.**

Stonehenge represents both great fear and great conviction. All this effort to circumscribe the gods, to insist that they listen and hear. Whether it's Stonehenge or pyramids in the Yucatán, Tiahuanaco

40. See 3.14.
41. See 3.11 (Face).

or Egypt, the whole society seems to roll its energies, its survival, into the construction. The primacy of that attempt at a stable relationship—humankind to God in the cosmos— is reflected in the magnitude of the stones. Floated down the river and dragged huge distances—this is the ultimate societal effort. **What stands from different periods is a good measure of how that culture valued what it built. What is made from stone and what from sticks tells the story.** Where are our old stones?

## PAR·IS

This comes from a city-planning book from the 1960s by Konstantinos Doxiades. It's the burgeoning urban geography of Paris—first a speck on an island in the Seine, growing rapidly onto both banks over a relatively short period of time. Do architects have the ability to evaluate the growth of cities and anticipate organizational solutions that would redirect that growth of cities to some intelligible form? Or **do planners inevitably run behind forces for which they can provide only a tentative exegesis in retrospect?** The urban theory is always behind the actual urban physiology, which continues to reformulate itself at a faster and faster pace. This is especially true of cities like Mexico City and Seoul and Manila and Taipei—cities that are not recognizable as identifiable parts of a coherent order and have no apparent starting or stopping parameters, just constant movement. A flood of elements shoved together and apart, growing and expanding, removing and replacing, amending and remodeling at an astonishing and exciting rate, a rate that is not controllable in a measured, systematic, methodological, sequential way. It's a growth that always outruns our ability to account for it. We need to discover a way to ride that wild chariot of the sun, and the jockey can't be Baron Haussmann any longer.

## PAT·FARD CLAY

This is a building designed by the architect I consider my real teacher. The architect is a man named Patfard Keatinge Clay. I met him when I was a student and he was a teacher at UC Berkeley. He worked in Le Corbusier's office in the late 1940s on the Marseilles Unité and Ronchamp. Then he came to the United States and was at Taliesen with Wright for a short period. Then he worked at Skidmore, Owings & Merrill in Chicago for a time. Then he started his own practice in San Francisco, which ran for maybe ten years. Later on he went to Spain. We've corresponded sporadically since.

The building is the student union at San Francisco State, a three-story concrete frame with triangular bays—lots of open space within the frame and various oddly shaped pieces that can be put in or taken away. The modern dictums, powerfully put. Conceptually there's the fundamental order, and then the more ephemeral programmatic parts are added or subtracted. At the top of the frame is a large open deck. The students can go up on the deck and relax, sit, or view. Out of the deck emerge two flying tetrahedrons, pointing to the sky. One contains a student lounge, and the other has group meeting spaces and a small theater with open seating accessible from the deck. The tetrahedrons emerge from the primary structure.

What I admire about the building is its audaciousness. It's a striking, beautiful form, unfettered by anything around it. The personal conviction that it was worthwhile to make this very particular kind of space object is remarkable for its time and place (perhaps for any time and place). Parenthetically, and a little bit sadly, I think the deck or the tetrahedrons (or one of the tetrahedrons) has been closed down because it wasn't designed to be accessible to the handicapped. Still, the project remains an extremely potent space for architecture and a clear attitudinal non sequitur, particularly in San Francisco. It was carried forward strictly by the conviction of the architect.

## THE PET·AL HOUSE

This is a photograph Tim Street-Porter shot from the Santa Monica freeway fifteen years ago. I always liked this photo—the house in the foreground against the background of those two towers in Century City. The plan form of the two towers is triangular and the pieces of the opened roof of the Petal House are also triangular, so there is, in one sense, something strangely similar about the two projects.

The photo is a dramatic representation of relative vantage points. From here the Petal House appears large and the towers small. How do projects of an imposing scale impact the city? What is the relation of size to impact? And how do we value the meaning of that small building against the kind of authority embodied by these enormous buildings?

## PHO·BOS

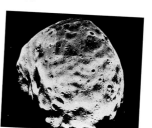

The Martian moon called Phobos interests me for several reasons. The image is beautiful, a precisely imprecise chunk of rock approaching a sphere but also moving away, floating in the ether. The moon rotates retrograde, so it rotates in the wrong direction according to the theories that were voguish when this discovery was made. So is there a wrong direction? According to the erstwhile Big Bang concept all the planets and the moons appeared at once, with similar ways of moving. **That theory, like many scientific theories (which are often represented as enduring as a consequence of the assumption that the conclusion is quantifiable), is likely to be replaced rather quickly by another, perhaps contrary hypothesis.** The social theories we could derive from crowd behavior in Berkeley[42] circa 1968, the allegiances and vilification of a caricatured opposition, might be more durable as laws, more dependable

42. See 3.6.

than our empirically derived scientific laws. The scientific dictums appear convincing for very short periods. Then, off to new theories somewhere else. This is the real nature of science's laws, distributed by what I would consider to be the only extant facsimile of a priesthood we have today. Phobos is not explainable as the scientists anticipated. And we'll never finally account for that empirically based subject matter. At that bottom there's no bottom.

## PRINCE OF WALES

A recent headline acknowledging the Prince of Wales and his "new" old school. Unfortunately, what's taught is often internalized by the learner and then spit out as if it were intrinsically so.

Certain people have the power to bring their ideas to bear in the world, including the Prince of Wales, who as a sponsor has the wherewithal to provide a curriculum and the fiscal solvency to open and sustain an educational institution where he and others can teach that the future is the past. I always thought his message was simply the message of a man who hadn't read enough Charles Dickens before advocating the memorializing of some of the most rancid tendencies in city building in the name of a disingenuous pseudo-progressive conservatism. And it's a failed resurrection: claiming the past is future won't work. **The prince has an apprehension of a crude contemporary arrogance that is a different flavor of brutality, though it is certainly possible, indeed necessary, to attack that glib modernism—but without resorting to Charles Dickens as the alternate city planner.**

## PROG·RESS

Faith in progress does not mean progress has occurred. That would be no faith.

Kafka doesn't rule out the possibility of an event happening that hasn't happened before and can't be referenced based on antecedents. The expression "faith in progress" is only representational of the "true" faith if it signifies a confidence that hasn't been sustained by a priori evidence. He doesn't think there is much evidence, but he doesn't want to say no progress, although probably his artistic instinct is "more of the same." This suggests the image of Kafka's man in *The Trial* facing the Door of the Law over many years, finally dying, and at the moment of death, seeing a light shining from underneath that inaccessible door. (Is the proposition "What hasn't happened is still possible, at least theoretically"?) **A successful conclusion, the possible occurrence of what seems inconceivable, is a dim but perpetual prospect. Gnostic architecture is that prospect.** We have all sorts of experiences that seem to suggest that life exists as an infinite number of disconnected snippets, and yet **there may be a way to jump over those disconnecteds to arrive at a different conclusion, to resolve rather than just dissect.**

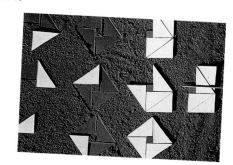

Lines drawn in the sand, illustrating the proportional properties of the Pythagorean theorem: the sum of the squares of the sides of the right triangle is equal to the square of the hypotenuse. Again the search for durable fundamental patterns. The essence proposed is mathematical and geometric—Pythagoras and Euclid dancing together. We're examining a subject that has long been fundamental to discussions on the content of architecture, to the ways of ordering buildings and the structure of cities. Pythagoras makes shapes we can write equations for, elements we can measure—right angles and squares. It is a quantifiable order, a measurable order with the conviction that a dimensional essence lies at the heart of things, not just at the heart of Pythagoras.

**Life qualified by quantifying.** We don't often acknowledge what Pythagoras's diagram has left out. In lectures I often use Rembrandt's painting *The Sacrifice of Isaac*[43] juxtaposed with this image in an effort to present another law and another voice, one that can't be reached with Pythagorean logic, analysis, or reading through an electron microscope—a kind of enigmatic "voice of God out of the whirlwind" law. The example was God's insistence that Abraham take his son to the mountain in Moriah and execute him. In the realm where Pythagoras makes sense, what Abraham was told by God might make no sense. I remember Kierkegaard's[44] discussion of the Abraham/Isaac story, and his rhetorical question "How many of you does this story keep up at night?" Apparently it kept Kierkegaard wide awake. Man exteriorizing man, apprehensive of that voice out of the whirlwind. Our culture has tried to insist there's only Pythagoras's voice. But the message to Abraham keeps appearing through the cracks in the right triangle.

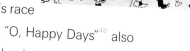

Innumerable Brooks Brothers[45] characters running madly after who knows what. This is what used to be referred to euphemistically as "the rat race." Hurrying mindlessly after Madison Avenue–determined goals. The extrovert's race as opposed to the introvert's race. The cartoon on the magazine cover, "O, Happy Days"[46] also deals with the homogeneity of suburban life—what values it values and what it omits.

One afternoon, a while ago, Malcolm Muggeridge, an Anglo-Catholic, was discussing totalitarianism with William F. Buckley on PBS. They were talking about this century's political and social leanings toward totalitarianism, and the tyranny of certain formulations of policy with respect to art and religion. Muggeridge referred to the totalitarian need to blot out all opposition, to cover the earth with concrete, metaphorically speaking; but the inevitable cracking of the concrete and, thus, the emergence from the cracks of Alexander Solzhenitsyn. Solzhenitsyn, at that time, was a symbol of resistance and the impossibility of imposing a final and complete tyranny.

43. See 5:8.
44. See 3.10 (Courage). See also 3.17.
45. See 3.7.
46. See 3.14.

### RAN I

A watercolor study by Akira Kurosawa for his movie *Ran*, which has, I think, been mistranslated as "chaos." Chaos is too simple for Kurosawa. Instead, there are always disconnected threads that sometimes vaguely imply the prospect of reconnection. The painting represents a scene at the end of the movie. The figure is blind, alone, standing at the edge of a cliff, about to tumble, with the world behind him on fire—spectacular but horrible. And the film delivers that same message. In existential terms, it's sad and disjointed. Not much hope, Pandora's box. But the prospect that the plan might succeed is there. The miss almost hits. **Perhaps the act of creating the film is itself the creative rejoinder to the film's emotional message.**

### RAN II

Here is Kurosawa's film rendition of the watercolor study from *Ran*. The same isolated character on the edge of the cliff, a silhouette, blind and moving with a cane to ward off disaster. Down below everything is burning. I don't want to leave the subject at the bottom of the cliff, though it's sometimes hard to get beyond that. Canetti's comment, "one shall seek nothingness only to find a way out of it"[47] applies here. Kurosawa's process of delivering this image is **an effort both to understand the emptiness and to climb over it,** perhaps through the art of the film itself. It is an effort to not simply disappear in a psychologically defoliated, physically demolished landscape.

### ROCK BUILD·ING

How to define the act of building? How to prescribe and proscribe the prospect? How to state the limits of architecture? What's a wall, a roof, a door, a floor? This is the rock building. This is the building rock. Nature made and now manicured? Or human-made and nature manicured? The object obviates any conventional definition.

### ROTH·KO

This is a painting from a series by Mark Rothko that has been critical to my interest in

47. See 3.10 (Conscience of Words). See also 3.11 (Dionysus and Apollo).

expressing the tension between alternative design possibilities occurring simultaneously, and the awareness that that dialectic might be transcended. But first, Rothko is an avant-gardist, attempting to modify the language of paint as the antecedent historic form loses its vitality. This reshuffling in form language can take place within a recognized grouping of signs and symbols, colors and techniques, or a novel framework might appear from outside the current representational methods. There's a mood in Rothko, a need that manifests itself in a constant effort to paint what is uniquely personal. At the same time, what intrigues me is the possibility that what he invented also has a generic sensibility. The discovery is both personal and generic. What Rothko conceived becomes another way, another plan, another pattern, and a contrary proposition to Tolstoy's[48] idea that history only exists one life at a time. Rothko's art history is both personal (private) and public (shared).

What I'm interested in postulating is a framework that bridges contrary ideas, a dialectical tension that might endure precisely because its allegiance is to a conceptual non-allegiance. The target is to embody the stress between allegiances. The Rothko painting, as an example, suggests two prospects. One is that of an orthogonal, or almost orthogonal, vantage point. That position starts with a Euclidean[49] discussion, a previously learned and therefore remembered geometry—one could write an equation for the rectangle, for the right angle. At the same time Rothko suggests a second prospect—the dissolution of the right angle. He shows both possibilities—the edges of the rectangle start to dissolve and suggest movement in another spatial direction, away from the rectangle we know toward a configuration less definable or yet to be defined. The painting is itself that tension between what we can recall of the orthogonal representation and away from that same representation. And therefore it embodies the stress by suggesting or proposing or embodying neither position entirely but both partially and simultaneously. **The painting is the dialectical tension in this exegesis.** If the painting is sufficiently powerful and the experience picks you up and carries you along then you live a vital transcendence for a moment.

## SAT•URN DE•VOUR•ING ONE OF HIS SONS

Goya originally painted this on the wall of his house. Now it's in the Prado. It is possibly the most horrifying object I've ever seen. To intellectualize it is to separate oneself from the horror. Saturn is time, not its symbol. Time devours us—ripping the head, swallowing the body. The subject matter is comparable to that character of Michelangelo's[50] staring at the skull. It's the experience Nietzsche[51] referred to when he talked about what breaks the will. The painting is the salvation of the artist's will.

48. See 3.32 (Triumph of Death).
49. See 3.14 (God the Geometer). See also 3.28 (School of Athens).
50. See 3.29 (Sistine Chapel).
51. See 3.11 (Dionysus and Apollo). See also 3.28 (Seven Sermons to the Dead).

## SCALE

What is the metaphorical meaning of the bent scale? Is objectivity numbered? Is empiricism simply dimension and quantity? What measures can measure measure? Not measure? What understanding does the scale contribute? What meanings does the scale omit? Can the bent scale measure what the straight scale cannot?

## THE SCH0OL OF ATH•ENS

A piece of a painting by Raphael in the Vatican Museum—man exteriorizing man. Plato, Aristotle, and Euclid[52]—the world as geometry. I've used that. I'm part of that. So I can also feel not only the self-confidence but the fear that the self-confidence might be misplaced. Man looks to attribute his methods to the investigation or discovery of an intrinsic order. A great statement of self-confidence—man can decipher the order. What was hidden is now revealed. Or is this just a prayer for the efficacy of the methods man invents?

## SEU•RAT

*Sunday Afternoon on the Island of La Grand Jatte,* painted at the end of the nineteenth century. The sociology of the painting is traditional, the Paris citizenry arrayed in the most orderly and well-behaved fashion, seated on the riverbank or on parade along the Seine. A clear acknowledgment of the conservative Parisian social pro forma. But simultaneously Seurat's method for applying paint—making the surface as an infinite number of almost distinct points—is a radical experimental technique that perhaps subverts the nominally well-behaved subject matter. So it is not a question here of a painter's prior allegiance to either an investigatory or a conventional representation; the one subsumes the other, recollecting forward.

## SEV•EN SER•MONS TO THE DEAD

I found the drawing, a Gnostic symbol of the early Christian era, in the book *Seven Sermons to the Dead* by Carl Jung. The head of a rooster means light, and the tail of a snake references dark. Light designates understanding and clarity, and, presumably, dark implies the opposite. Abraxas signifies both oppositions and the reconciliation of oppositions. Nietzsche's Dionysus and Apollo[53] defined oppositions but not the reconciliation. Yin and yang convey a similar meaning in a

52. See 3.14 (God the Geometer). See also 3.26 (Rothko).
53. See 3.11. See also 3.27 (Saturn Devouring One of His Sons).

more abstract graphic language.

The Gnostic life is personal, and not transferable. This isn't an ideology that can be learned and applied collectively. Understanding occurs one person at a time. Perhaps it's possible to bridge the light and dark conflict, to resolve the dichotomy. **The Gnostic experience, in spatial terms, transcends the intellectual dialectic but doesn't eradicate it. The contention of intellectual possibilities—dark and light—remains. Abraxas makes a transcendent prospect available.**

SIS·TINE CHA·PEL

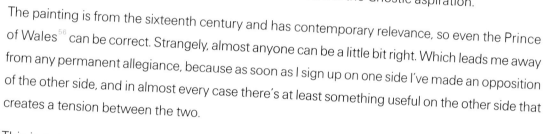

In this portion of the back wall of the Sistine Chapel, Michelangelo looks at his future and everyone else's. In the Western sense, it's the fundamental existential problem of the limits of everything, very much the focus of the intellectual history of the twentieth century, whether it's Cage[54] or Schoenberg or Joyce[55] or Genet. I don't know whether architecture has ever explicitly made that subject its subject: how fragile the experience of living is, one life at a time. Building that life-tension into architecture is the Gnostic aspiration.

The painting is from the sixteenth century and has contemporary relevance, so even the Prince of Wales[56] can be correct. Strangely, almost anyone can be a little bit right. Which leads me away from any permanent allegiance, because as soon as I sign up on one side I've made an opposition of the other side, and in almost every case there's at least something useful on the other side that creates a tension between the two.

This is not an argument for not making a choice, but it is an argument for skepticism about any position held too tightly for too long. Maybe that's where the fear is. Maybe Michelangelo's image might account for the Prince of Wales's backward reverence, as he looks over his shoulder, desperate for a durability that could stand in opposition to that ephemeral human condition painted on the Sistine wall. The Eastern vantage point is different. Underneath change and movement is something still that is no thing. How to name that, how to touch that without contaminating it? Both experiences are real, both the change and movement (which feels more poignant to me) and the stillness. If I'm conscious that there is another possibility that could exist beyond the terror and panic on this face, then my retort to Michelangelo could be "What is all the fuss about?"

SKEL·E·TON

All the pieces intact. Reassembled so the surface configuration is implied by the substructure. Or is it? **A question of the relationship of support to surface to meaning. Outside to inside.** How are they associated? Outside observed on the inside, inside observed on the

54. See 3.7.
55. See 3.16.
56. See 3.24. See also 3.18 (Lenin).

3.29

outside? Rules for the expression of support to surface? Hierarchy of support parts? A *Helmet*[57] of sorts.

### SLOW•NESS

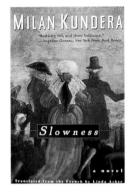

In his novel, Milan Kundera suggests not racing to the next thing and the next thing and the next thing and on and on to no thing. Our culture seems to create preferences and immediately discard them. We can't sustain a focus. We're never satisfied; there is no final. Nothing completes. It's always the anticipated next thing, and that makes each current experience ephemeral and insufficient. There is never a completed aspiration, never an arrived-at destination. The destination is simply the next destination.

I don't want to say that I understand slowness, but I think that I understand speed. What I wanted to do in the epigram was to put the two together and suggest a very different possibility. Marinetti, at the beginning of the century, set a behavior pattern, and Kundera suggests something quite different at the end of the century. Maybe we had to go through Marinetti to arrive at Kundera.

### TAT•LIN

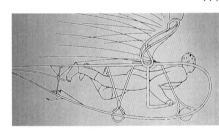

Russian constructivism and Tatlin's glider. The magic and majesty of flight. Daedalus and Icarus[58] becoming technically plausible in the 1920s. How fascinating that what is so compelling about technological advances is only briefly compelling. The wonder at the achievement is as important as the technology. Should a 1,500-foot-high tower or an airplane traveling 700 miles an hour or a bridge spanning 1,500 feet not be an enduring astonishment? And all of that done by insignificant man, whose efforts the trees devoured at Angkor Wat.[59] Perhaps the time span of a single life is inadequate to measure the durability of a particular technical achievement. **Perhaps that magnitude is only measurable after the utilitarian purposes are lost or obscured.**

From a second vantage point it's curious that a conceptual trail runs from the form language of constructivism through the form language of deconstructivism. Russian constructivism, with an ethos of technical optimism and historic progress, points, quizzically, to deconstructivism with its perpetual fragments and loss of hope.

### TI•A•HUA•NA•CO

A gargantuan archaeological piece of unknown origin in Bolivia. The contemporary nomenclature refers to this structure as the Tower of the Sun. It adjoins Lake Titicaca, where a once

57. See 3.15.
58. See 5:11.
59. See 3.4. See also 3.7 (Buddha).

mighty civilization apparently lies under water. This is a poignant example of forces in history that our conceptions don't yet, and may never, have the capacity to account for. It's very, very old, in historical terms. A colossal cut-stone construction. The scale is astonishing. There it is, powerful and mute. The enigma of history. **The building is pre-Maya, pre-Inca, pre-everybody as far as we know, which isn't sufficiently far to catalog the builders accurately in our perpetually amended historical chronology.** For all our culture's eloquence of information, of knowing, and our rhetoric of understanding, when we stand in the face of Tiahuanaco we feel not only its majesty but the inadequacies of our ways of accounting for it.

## TIAN·AN·MEN SQUARE

The Tiananmen Square event fascinated me—listening to the rhetoric and watching the unabashed brutality of totalitarian power, and hearing brute draconion power represented as honorable and the opposition as diabolical.

I can remember a crowd of ten thousand one day in Sproul Plaza on the Berkeley campus,[60] with numberless people speaking vociferously, some eloquently, over a public microphone, criticizing the administration of the university (with justification) and congratulating themselves on their ability to intervene in the university's history in the interests of justice, democracy, and freedom. Then one guy got up—I remember he had red hair and a black patch over his left eye. This is 1965. And when he started to speak he was booed. There wasn't much patience with his sympathies, which were outside the predictably narrow range of campus allegiances. Heroes and villains seemed predetermined—not much dexterity of mind and opinion. I could see immediately that certain ambiguities, certain tensions would be lost in the face of the apparent need to polarize positions and insist on the purity of the student vantage point. So this guy with the eye patch jumped up and started talking from the perspective of persecuted students in Romania. He was a graduate student. He spoke about big black cars coming around corners in Bucharest, and secret police grabbing people off the streets, dragging them into the cars, never to be seen again. Suddenly Bob Dylan's "Sad-Eyed Lady of the Lowlands" blared over the loudspeakers. I can't recall any objections to the censoring of a student who had fought tyranny in another place.

Testing the belief system is always tough. If an entrenched, established position has to be moved it always resists. I wonder sometimes in discussions with clients and city administrators if the argument and intelligence of particular positions is only a veneer for the relative power positions of the people involved in the discussion. **What appears to be a debate about alternate solutions is likely to be decided on the basis of relative power positions, not content,** and that is well understood and needn't be stated explicitly. What I love about this anonymous man in front of the tank is the possibility of standing against that force and causing a retreat—a revision. The man stood for a moment, held his position in the face of the tank, and the tank went around. Architecture can sometimes obligate the tyrant to retreat.

## TRI•UMPH OF DEATH

A Brueghel painting. Here the subject of death is not a general matter but specific to each individual. The painting is enormously complicated. It reminds me of Tolstoy's[61] conception of the writing of history: there is no composite history, no single direction, only private histories. Only individual renditions. What's real for Tolstoy is what runs through the life of an infinite number of people, person by person. So to tell the painting's story is to tell it story by story, but in what order? From the top, the side, all at once? The discussion in *War and Peace* of the battle of Borodino is quite different from that same subject studied as a chapter in military history at West Point. The military academy historians would conclude that for tactical reasons the cavalry went here and the infantry went there and the terrain was like this and the battle proceeded according to such and such a narrative sequence. That is, the battle is a manifestation of a sequence of reciprocal tactical decisions. But Tolstoy represents it from the vantage point of the individual cavalryman, in a ditch, fallen from his horse in the midst of smoke, fire, and mud. There is no suprapersonal West Point pro forma; only the confused lives of the participants, one by one; only discontinuity. And it's disingenuous, says Tolstoy, to overlay an order, an intellectualization, a nomenclature, a map. This relative of vantage point is famously portrayed in Akira Kurosawa's[62] *Rashomon*. I know that some conceptual overlook contributes to the understanding of both Borodino and *Triumph of Death*. But it would be a mistake to ignore Tolstoy's perception that the history of an event can be told only person by person. Including that hypothesis tends to mitigate the single conclusions requisite to a larger vision.

## TUR•NER

In this painting by Turner, done early in the nineteenth century, the fog is descending, or ascending. One can't determine. The enigma or mystery arrives in Turner's astonishing ability to abrogate the definition of what one sees through the use of color. But this is no single color we could name.[63] Turner's colors are light striking wet after a storm. The colors are complex beyond words, suggesting a number of perceptual possibilities. The subjects at sea are partly legible, partly illegible; and that ambiguity allows the imagination to consider what the fog might be covering, what it might disclose if it lifted. Of course there are lurking monsters[64] in the water. There's a Paul Klee[65] painting, not dissimilar, with the man in that peculiar boat spearing two sea monsters. Does the clear view always reveal monsters? Or is there always some fog under the fog?

65. See 3.18.

61. See 3.27 (Rothko).
62. See 3.26 (Ran). See also 5:11.
63. See 1.9–10. See also 5:4.
64. See 3.15 (Hybrid Monster). See also 3.18 (Lurking Monster).

UX·MAL

I took this photograph standing on the mislabeled Pyramid of the Magician looking out into that infinite green. The jungle is ravenous in the Yucatán. Far away there's a piece of a pyramid and, I suspect, other buildings, even cities that could be scraped clean. **Architecture keeps moving, not always in the direction you would like.** But it's irrepressible. We keep building. But what's also irrepressible is what keeps devouring the buildings. Doctor Doolittle's Push Me Pull You, incognito, perpetually metamorphosing.

# 4

# OUTSIDE OF THE INSIDE

What you've got as an initial scheme is a series of small blocks, strapped together to prevent their busting out at the seams. And the straps or seams double as supports: columns or beams.

There's the big block in the air, with no lateral support in either direction. California is obviously earthquake territory, and when columns supporting the block began to appear, I could anticipate that some bracing would be required. It's unusual in California, or anywhere on the Pacific rim, to build a building and lift it in the air without shear walls going to the ground. But the need to retain the truck access on the road suggested elevating the block.

The dotted lines begin to explain the positioning of the girders spanning the road under the building, relative to the bracing. What I developed was a girder system where each member is dimensionally identical to the next and, at the same time, a variable, flexible structure that responds to column supports at different centers.

At the top is the first look at an asymmetrical girder configuration, supporting the blocks as a response to the varying roof profiles of the two buildings adjoining the road—flat roof at the west and shed roof at the east—and a desire to let sunlight into the space under the block. There was some consideration that the walkway/roadway would be glazed, that is, that glass would extend between the roof of the existing buildings and the soffit of the new building over the road. That idea was ultimately abandoned.

There is also the first decisive articulation of the first anomaly, the first spatial exception to the block. It hasn't yet migrated to the corner of the block; it's just a volumetric idea. And the legs have a somewhat different character than the columns in the final solution. But all the elements are there.The spatial concept has a relationship to a drawing I did twenty years ago for Stanley Tigerman's Late Entries to the Chicago Tribune Tower Competition. It has the aspect of an hourglass, both externally and figuratively, but it's people, not sand, that flow vertically through the spaces.

The small drawing of a square with diagonal elements looks like a diagram of the roof of the building at Leicester by James Stirling. He actually took a skylight glazing system and turned it forty-five degrees in plan. What's astonishing is the intersection of that forty-five-degree sloped glazed roof with the orthogonal walls. Beautiful. I don't know whether I was thinking about that here; I don't know if I had just visited the building. I can't tell you what specifically that project has to do with the Samitaur building. It seems to have no direct visible connection, but Stirling's sensibility should be acknowledged.

The sketch with the horizontal slabs hypothesizes a different way of dealing with the block, different from wrapping the blocks or holding the blocks together in the plane of the wall. The concern with the small blockish pieces being put together was their spatial viability—how would they be occupied? What do the block dimensions mean? If they actually mean interior walls, then the spaces are too tiny and discontinuous. You can't get from one to the next, so the idea of pieces as volumes or solids becomes the idea of pieces indicated just at the skin: planes, not volumes.

4.1

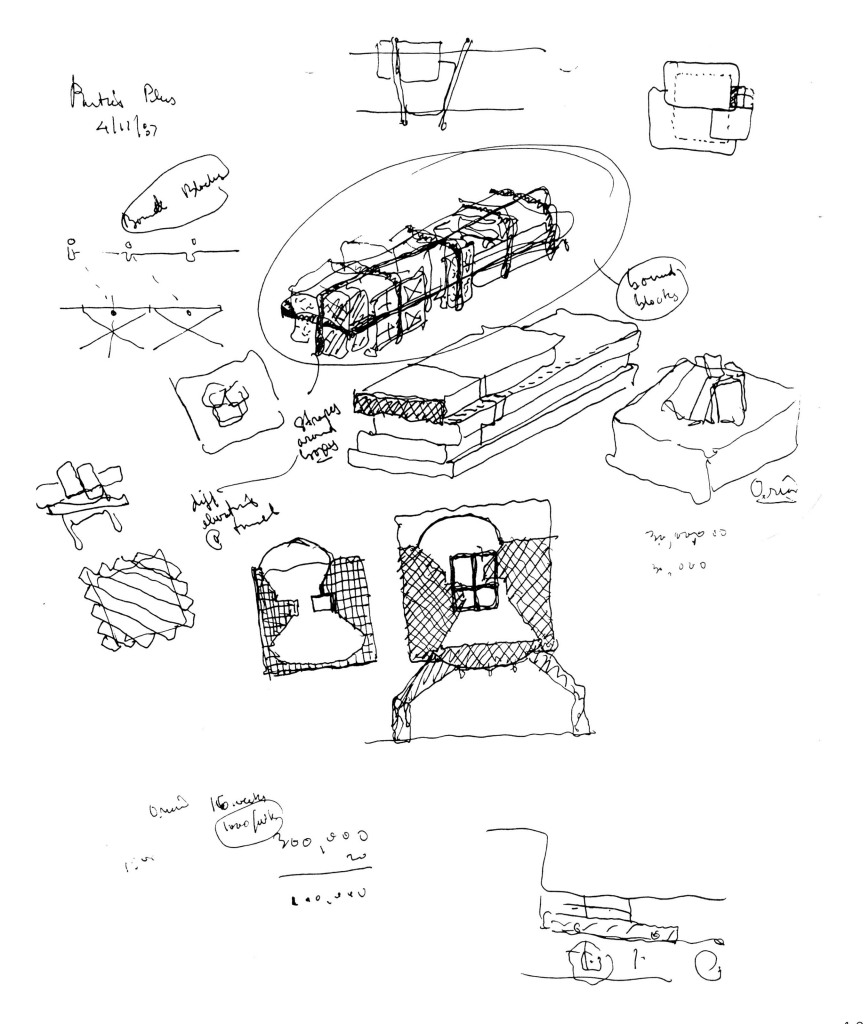

4.2

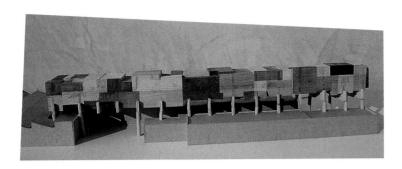

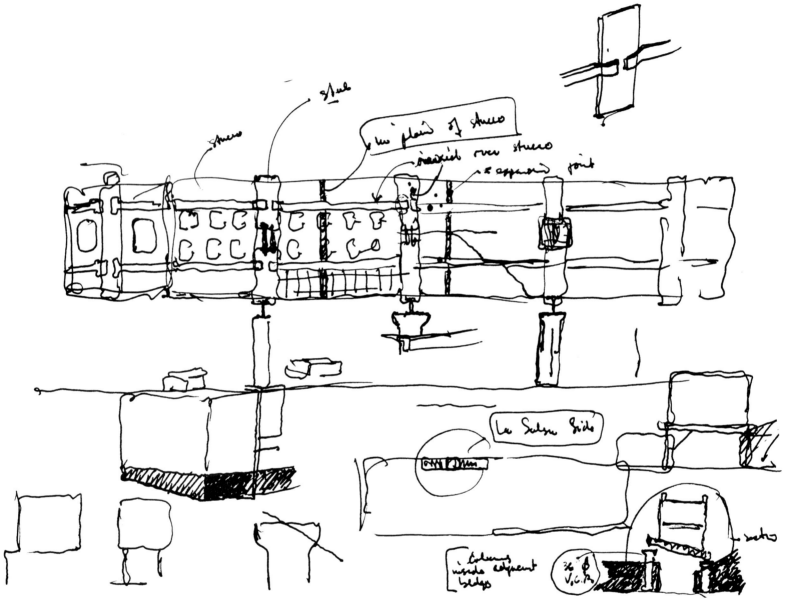

These sketches investigate the question of the strap and its possible relation to a glazing system, and suggest a design for a punched-window system with two openings of different sizes. One window may be double-height—two floors. There would have to be a double-height space—omitting the third floor on occasion—to make sense of this glass system. The hatched area represents a particular wall surface that curves under the main building and forms part of the soffit. Above the curve is a horizontal strap. And a vertical strap intercepts it. The prospect of the straps strapped together, extending vertically up and over the top, down the other side, and under the bottom of the block is suggested. That idea was further developed in later drawings of the soffit over the entry road. It looks here like the straps coincide with a proposed column structure. The large straps on the face of the wall appear to extend to intersect the columns below.

4.3

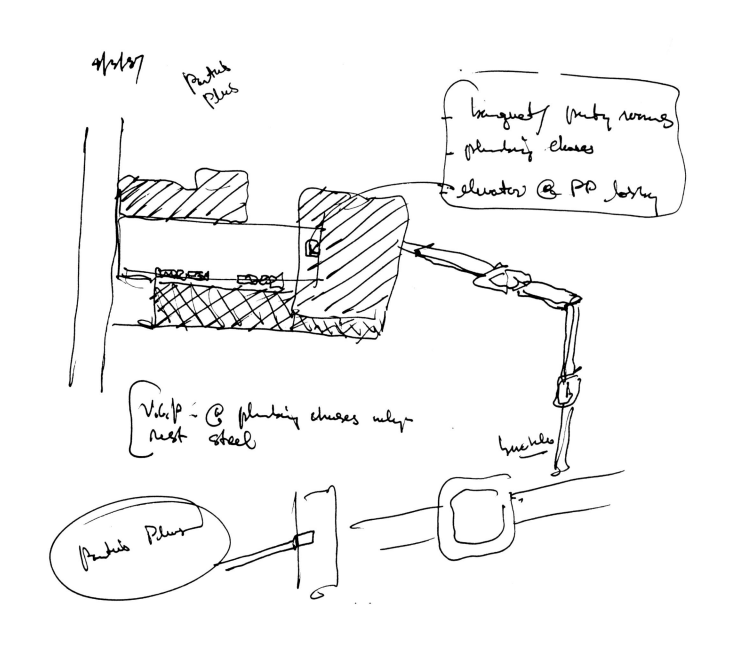

The text and connecting line locate the elevator in plan. The lobby is at the end of the road adjoining the elevator core.
Here again is the buckle, the joining of the strap pieces, conceived to hold the exterior panels together conceptually.

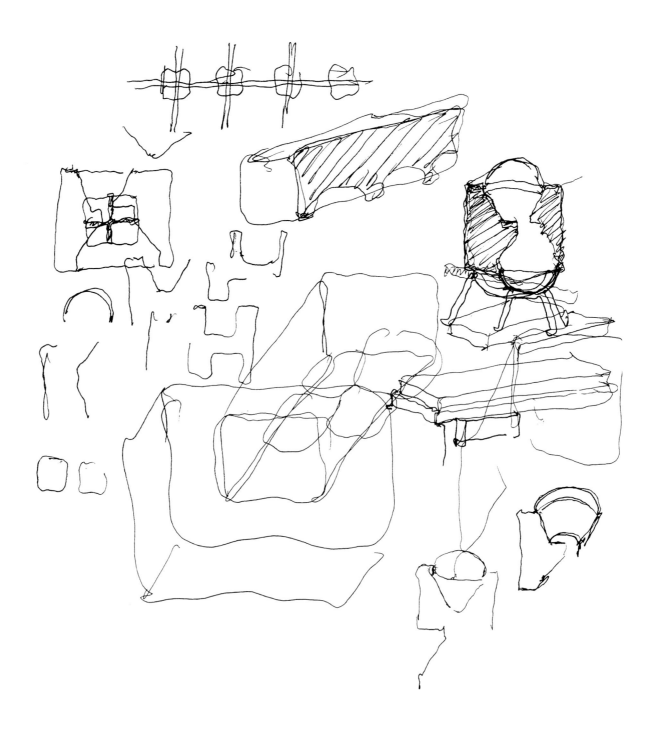

There's an important section at the north end of the block—the floor and a floor-and-a-half-high boardroom, with great views of Santa Monica and the ocean out the west wall; the Hollywood hills, the Santa Monica freeway, Westwood, and Century City to the north; and downtown to the east—a great way to decipher L.A. The floor-to-floor heights were tightly limited by the city's forty-five-foot height limit above and the fourteen-foot six-inch truck clearance on the road below. There were two interior exceptions made, two breaks in the office floors: one was the double-height lounge/bathroom space in the center of the building, with the five-foot diameter steel bathroom cylinders (the diameter a consequence of the handicapped wheelchair turnaround requirement); the other was the boardroom.

The conceptual hourglass discussion is resurrected, shown here together with the straps—an attempt to integrate the strapping system with what came to be the entry stair. It's starting to work its way into the block corner. Originally it was drawn on the street elevation. And the girder support system and the slope of the girder across the road show up here in conjunction with the soffit over the road.

The aqueduct idea, another gesture in the process of defining the base of the block, disappeared (fortunately) except at the bridge area under the second anomaly (the pool) where two columns were omitted for truck egress and a long span was required.

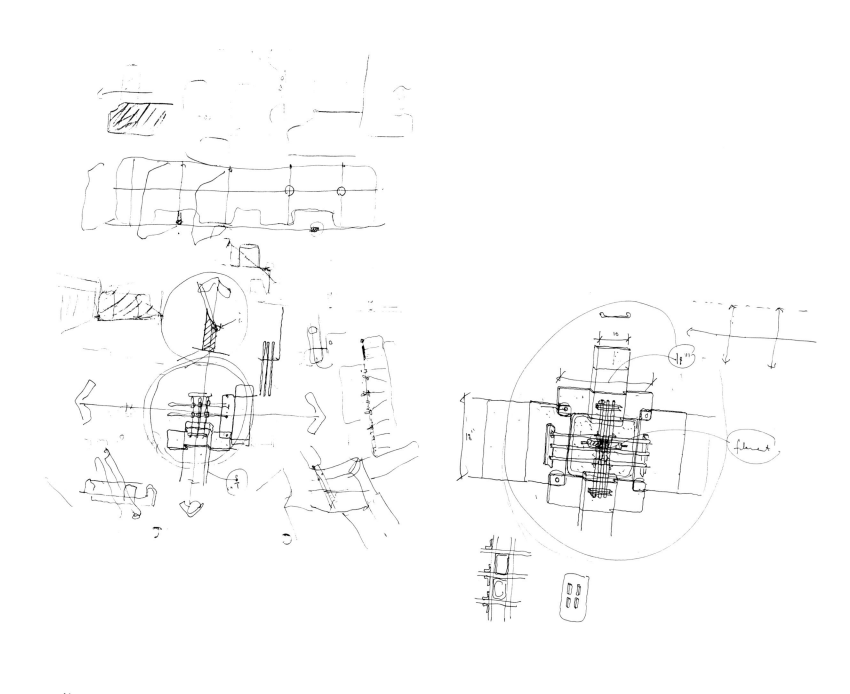

Here's a detail designed to resist the prospect of the exploding kiln (the source of the strap idea). There's also a very unusual detail at the parapet edge of the block, as finally designed. The conventional sheet-metal cap at the top of the wall is omitted. The transition from wall to cap—from vertical to horizontal—is mitered, so the exterior wall appears to go right up to the sky. Just flying green block and that's it. No sheet-metal cap. Instead, the top of the wall is plaster.

Here again the additive wall components are only on the surface; no longer are there three-dimensional blocks that, in the aggregate, make up the raised building. There's also a suggestion that interior walls could originate on lines determined by the wall panel system. The association is between a joint and the possible position of an interior wall.

The intersection of the vertical and horizontal straps that were to restrain the bursting blocks (which became the raised single block) looks like a city plan by Ledoux. It's dead symmetrical—and can be read at a small or large scale. There's a segmented vertical steel strap, a central plate, and a segmented horizontal strap. There was once a light proposed behind the steel bars that cross in the center. The straps occur in different planes with different thicknesses overlaying one another. So there is one strap system running around the blocks like a sort of package wrapping, and another wrapping the block ninety degrees from the first. Because the straps overlap each other, they're fastened at the corners of the intersection. What's going on here is perhaps obsessive (which is not necessarily pejorative). Then there are the raised bars crossing at the intersection of horizontal and vertical straps. It looks like you could consider building the straps and forget about the rest of the building.

The boardroom raised over the existing sawtooth roof is also shown here but not yet with the floor-and-a-half height.

In the center of the sketch is a ceiling plan showing the girders at the soffit over the road.

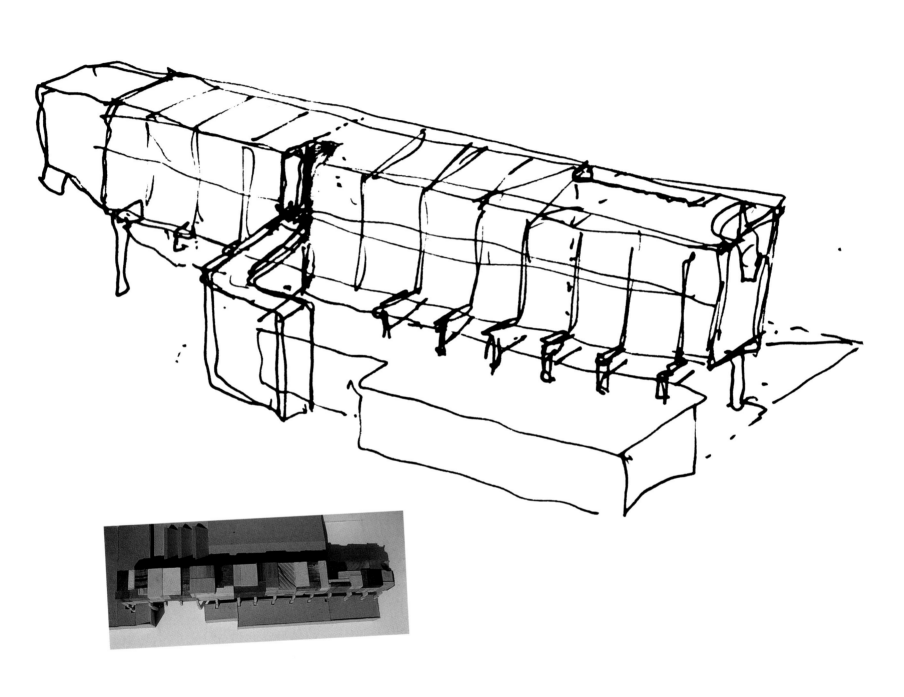

In this series of sketches, the general configuration of the raised building is defined—its position relative to the existing structures on the ground (the metal shed and the brick building) and the position of the two anomalies, the entry stair and the pool. And you can see the columns here, and the girders under the block supported on columns coming out of the roofs of the existing buildings. The instinct is to never quite accept the discipline of the block without offering an alternative to it.

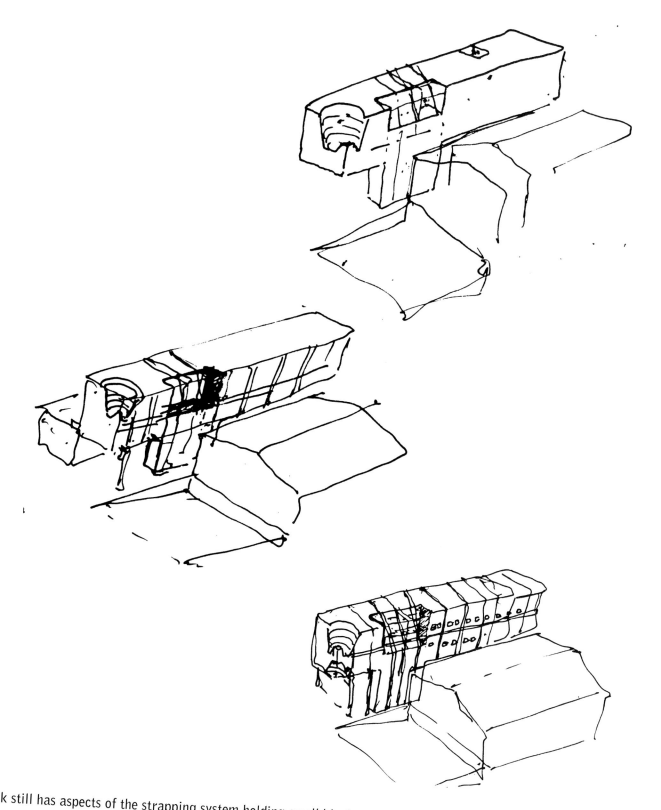

The block still has aspects of the strapping system holding small blocks together to form the large block, but the block is no longer a series of irregular pieces; the divisions in the block are now more regular. Although the joints are still shown crossing the top of the roof, the delicate plaster-stop system that was eventually used in the elevation of the building begins to be suggested.

The cut for the first anomaly, the entry stair, is in the corner now but hasn't yet gone all the way through the building. It's just a cutout on the second floor, and the resolution at the ground is missing.

You can see some kind of bleacher seating with a view to La Cienega. The bleacher, which later becomes the double-height interior lounge, and the indentation on the west side, which later becomes the pool, are identified here as design subjects, but not yet resolved.

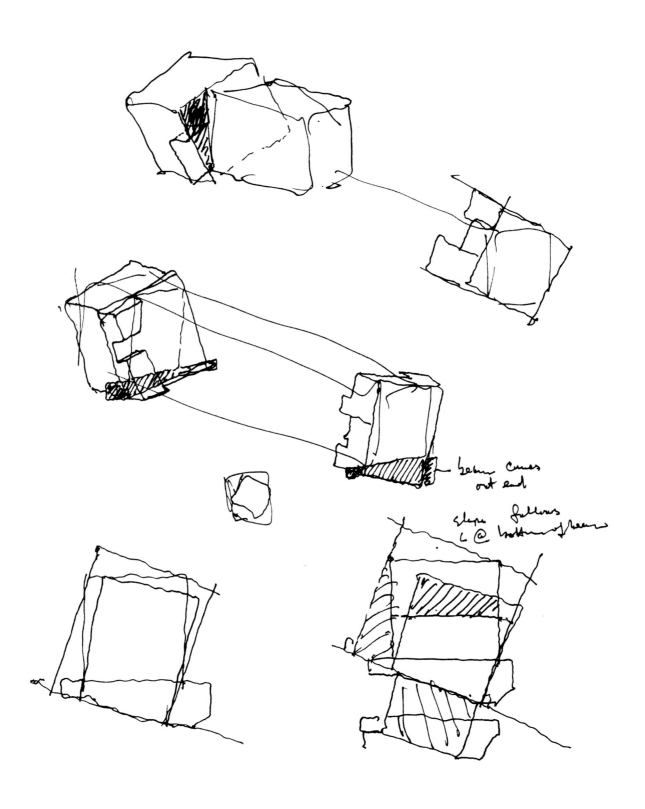

This shows an alternate conception of the building block in the air. It has the big girder support. It examines the orthogonal block and starts to speculate on whether the frame above the girders could move or rotate. There would be an evolving

4.9    sequence of possible block positions. This is another conceptual option.

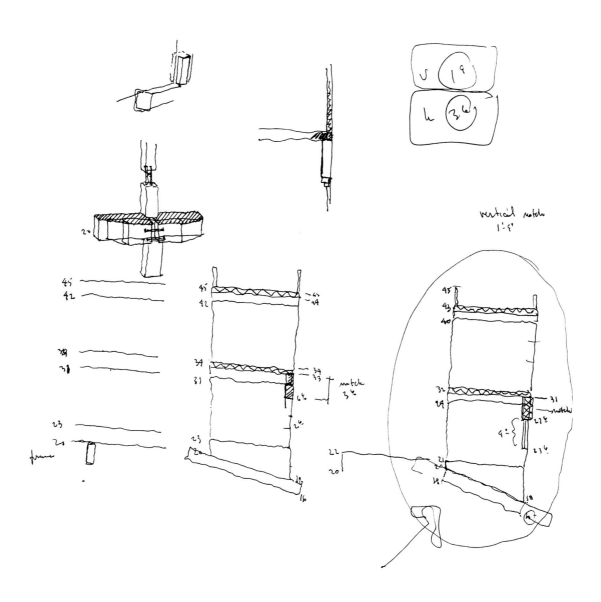

This series is concerned with dimensional issues. The circled section indicates that this was my conclusion in establishing floor-to-floor and floor-to-ceiling heights.

What I'm careful to accommodate under the building is the vertical clearance: a fire truck requires fourteen feet six inches clear to the bottom of the girder, according to L.A. regulations. The height limit stated in the L.A. zoning code in the area was forty-five feet. (In Samitaur 3, I have designed two 235-foot high-rises under a newly revised code, revisions instigated by the first phase.) In Samitaur 1, we were pushed from the bottom and from the top. In between we had to fit two office floors.

The width of the office block was also limited by the Los Angeles Fire Department, which wouldn't allow the building to extend over the existing buildings on either side of the road. So the site became the width of the road only. That made the block thirty feet wide.

4.10

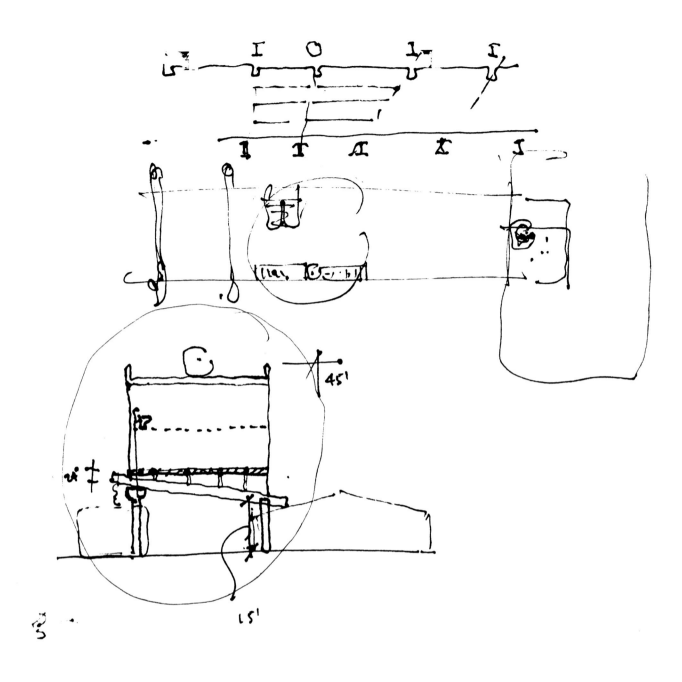

Another speculation on the location of columns. And there was a question of stiffeners on the girders: the concern that the girders remain identical while accommodating different shear-stress circumstances (the purpose of the stiffeners). The question of how the block will be supported is still open here. At this point it looks like two beams, one horizontal, one inclined, with intermediate supports. Not one big girder—more like a truss.

There's another subject suggested (circled in the middle of the sketch) but not resolved—how to recognize the entry/exit stairs. One of the principles in the building is that there are no spaces that are simply what they are in a utilitarian sense. So a stair is never simply a stair. The first anomaly indicates the entrance and incorporates a stair and a deck. Similarly, the second anomaly weaves the stair into that exterior space which holds a fountain and bridge. There's also a very intricate exit stair adjacent to the lobby that in section works its way from the existing sawtooth building at grade up into the new building block. We had to work our way past the elevator core and negotiate two sectionally different buildings in two plan positions in order to get the stair to fit. It's more an adventure in exiting than simply a stair.

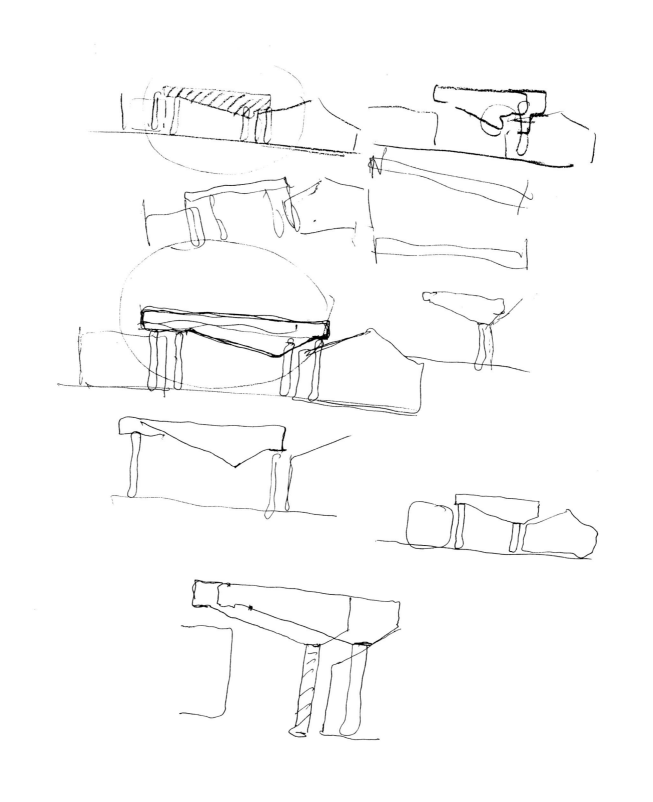

This sketch examines the relationship of natural light on the road under the building to the position of the existing brick and corrugated-steel buildings. There was a concern that the girder profile not block the light entering between the new building above and the old buildings below. The girders extend horizontally over the adjacent buildings, and the sloped roof of the metal shed can't touch the girders. The shed is on the east side of the road and the brick building on the west. The column is outside the wall in the road or within the space of the old buildings. The girders sit on the columns as the columns project from the roofs or stand in the road adjacent to the existing building walls. But you can see the girder profile being studied, different ways of configuring the girder, always with the concern of letting the light in at the edge of the road and not bumping the existing roofs.

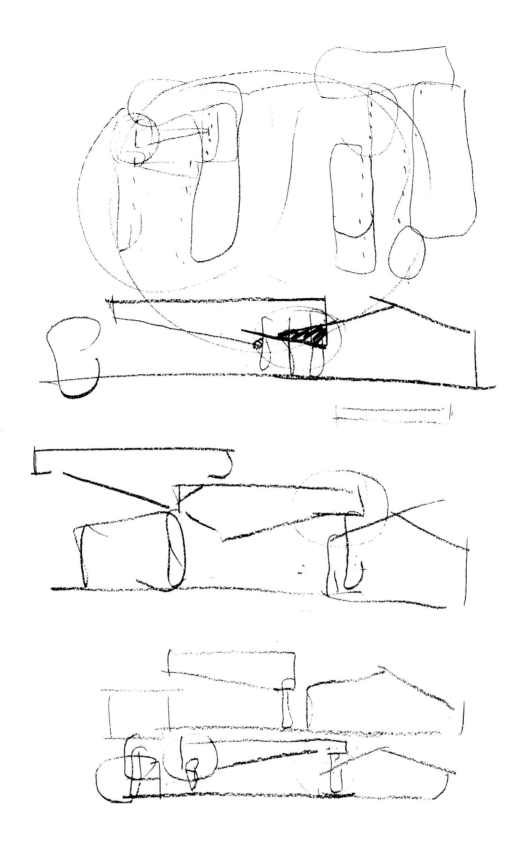

The issue of shape and position of girders and columns is considered here again. This was a potentially intriguing variation. It never got very far. But it had to do with the possibility that the columns could rotate and spin the attached girder over the existing building, so that the air space over the road would no longer limit the site. Just another permutation that couldn't be pursued because of the zoning limitations on the site.

It also looks like I'm still considering the building as a number of distinct sectional pieces. The sketch investigates how the block could grow differently, possibly winding up outside the defined site. This also proposes reusing the column/girder idea on the second level.

4.13

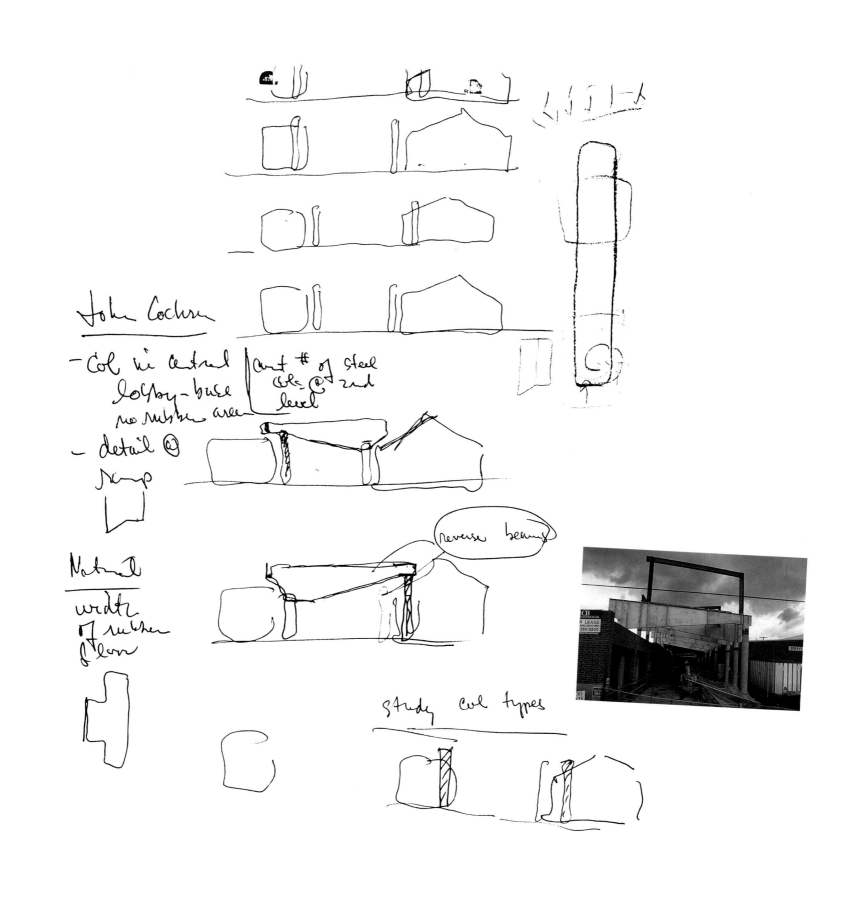

John Cochran

– Col in central
lobby–but
no ... area

art # of steel
cols @ 2nd
level

– detail @
ramp

Natural

width
of rubber
floor

reverse bearing

study col types

Columns in the old buildings adjacent to the road; columns out of the old buildings adjacent to the road.

This is the only drawing that actually shows the girders in two opposing positions as they span the road—one with the heavy end on the west, the other with the heavy end on the east. And this is what actually happened—the girder position reversing, depending on the profiles of the roofs of the old structures adjoining the road.

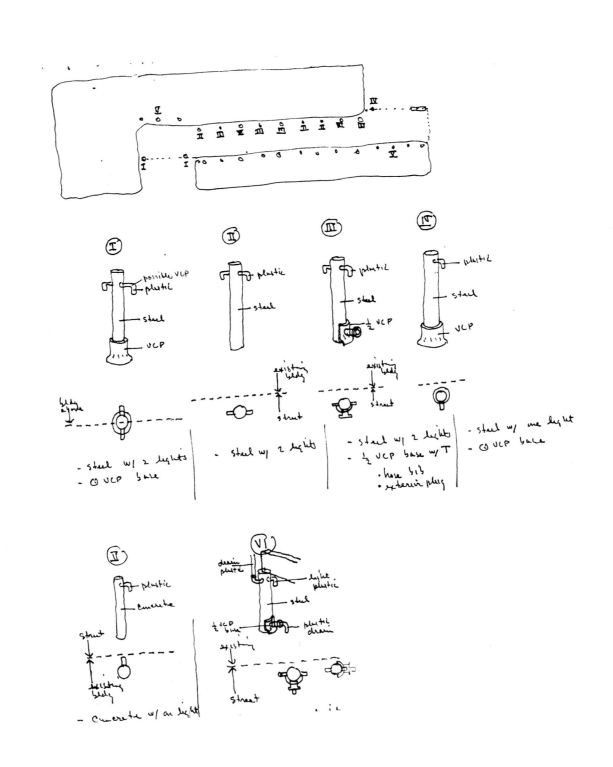

The columns as structural supports are here defined secondarily by issues of utility: power, drainage, protection from passing cars. This is one of a number of studies of additional uses of the steel-pipe columns. First, the pipe columns have, for structural reasons, two different diameters—eighteen inches and twenty-four inches. Second, the columns might be defined by other than support considerations—rigid frames and diagonal bracing. Third, the columns fall in the road or in the adjacent buildings. Different column types, uses, and locations. The specifics of each column would start to obviate the conception of the column as a simple support rule and make it harder, by intention, to understand the operational structural proposition. What I have done here is locate and number every column on the road. The north end of the brick building has a solid face on the road. The south end has big doors and windows facing the interior street. Columns are placed outside the building in the road on the north end and inside the building on the south, adjacent to the existing piers. Columns are located outside the metal shed, but inside the plaster sawtooth building adjoining the shed to the north. There's a very thorough evaluation here of the different columns and alternate column locations, all related to changes of circumstance on the site and/or a variety of utilitarian purposes. In the final design, the two column diameters and the locations of columns in and out of the old buildings were retained, but the other distinctions were omitted.

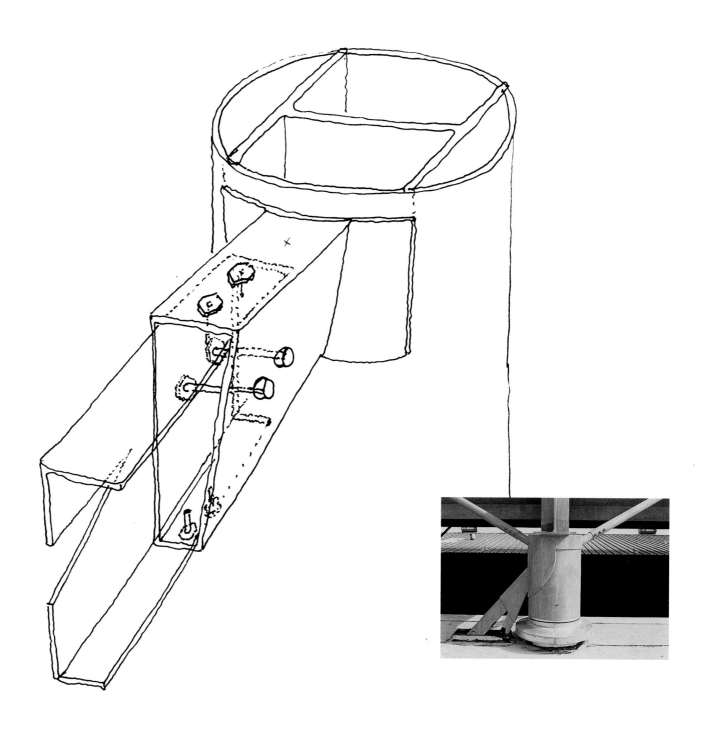

This is a construction detail of the pipe-column girder supports and cross-bracing to resist wind and earthquake forces. The structure had to be braced in the long (north-south: 320 feet) and short (east-west: 30 feet) directions. The rigid frames in the short direction all have moment connections. There are five moment frames serving that purpose in the building. Then in the long direction diagonal bracing between the frames is used at the road level. Typically, in California, walls extend from roof to foundations, but the only walls that follow that precedent here are the elevator core walls. The rigid-frame pipe columns have structural steel Is within the pipes. The Is were attached to the girders. A steel plate was welded to each column face to which the diagonal brace, a steel angle, was attached. There are a number of problems we resolved related to the positioning of two different angles crossing each other and intersecting in the same vertical plane.

4.16

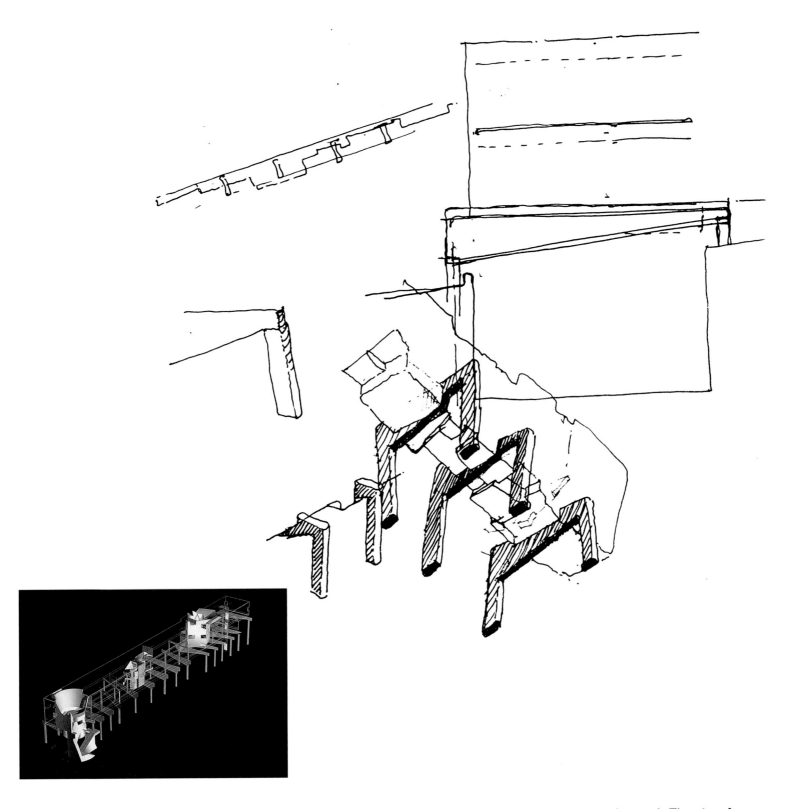

This is a worm's-eye perspective, looking up from under the road at the feet of the columns in the road. The view from underneath allows you to understand the relationship of the columns and girders to the underside of the raised block and the configuration of the ceiling over the road. In these propositions the multiple blocks appear again. The underside, the soffit, is made up of orthogonal blocks of different sizes, and the girders subtend and give way to the ceiling form. The underside of the building is rising and falling with right-angle strips. The undersides of the girders here seem to be horizontal, parallel to the plane of the road, very different from the final resolution.

There is another condition here that ameliorates the final block in the air—that amends it. The soffit over the road sometimes curves at the transition from ceiling to wall. I'm not sure I would do that again. Maybe another year (eleven years to build instead of ten) and that curve would have come out, too. I originally thought of associating a curve at the block edge with letting more light into the road area (between the soffit and the old roof edge). At one time there was also the possibility of indicating access doors to the buildings adjoining the road being indicated with a curve in the vertical/horizontal transition above.

4.17

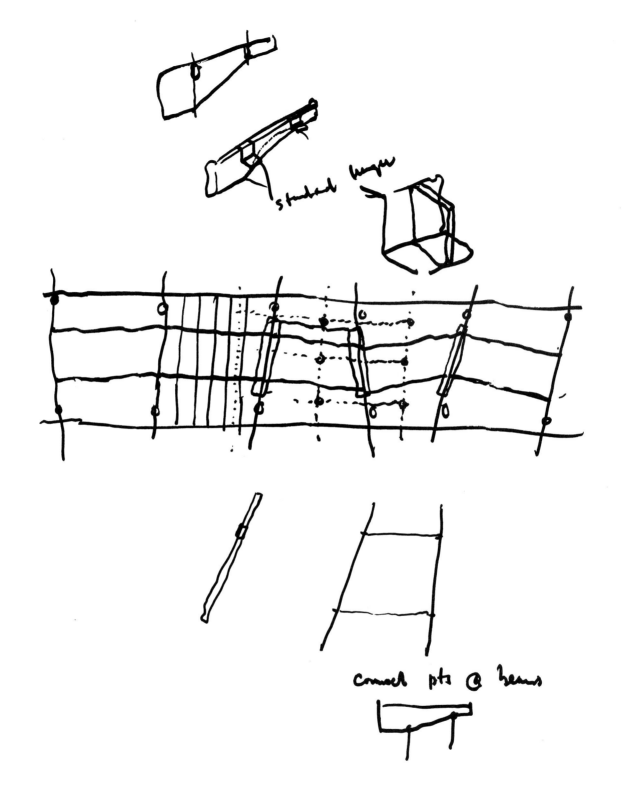

This drawing shows the positioning of girders and secondary beams in the ceiling over the road. The secondary beams span between the girders, which sit on the pipe columns.

It also illustrates the points of connection on the faces of the girders that locate the secondary beams and divide the soffit into three sections. The intermediate beams are not really beams but were thought of as visible surrogates for the next step in a legible sequence of structure (which is actually buried in the ceiling).

And there's another area of decision here that involves locating sprinklers and lights in the ceiling. The soffit had to be sprinkled to achieve the required fire rating on the road. There was also the issue of lighting that space. In the end, I pulled all the lighting off the soffit; the ceiling is now lit from the roofs of the buildings adjacent to the road.

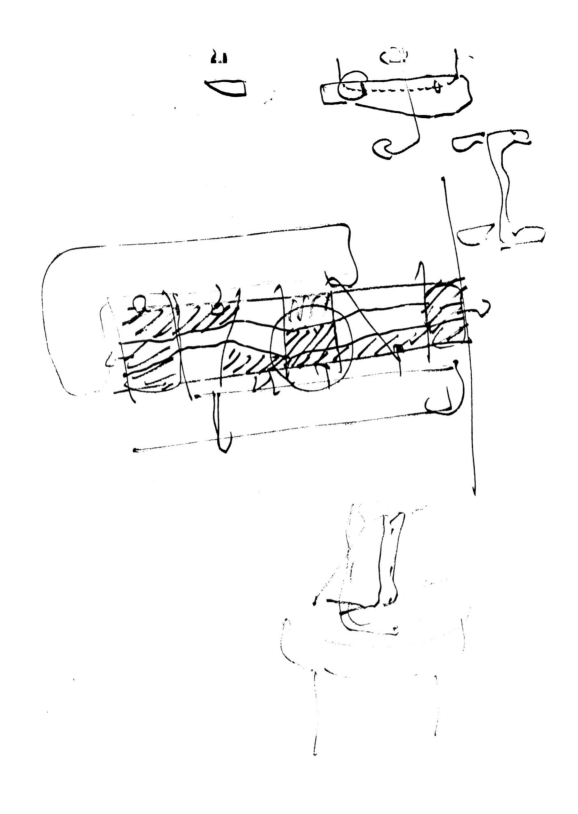

This is a useful diagram because it deals with a lot of issues simultaneously: columns that are inside, columns that are outside, girders, intermediate beams between girders, and the location of curving soffits. The order of smaller beams running between the girders segregates the soffit into three zones per bay. The curved ceiling starts and stops at the intermediate beams. The ceiling between the two smaller beams is always horizontal, and the section between the beam and the edge of the block curves when the building actually goes beyond the road and extends over entrances to the old sawtooth shed.

4.19

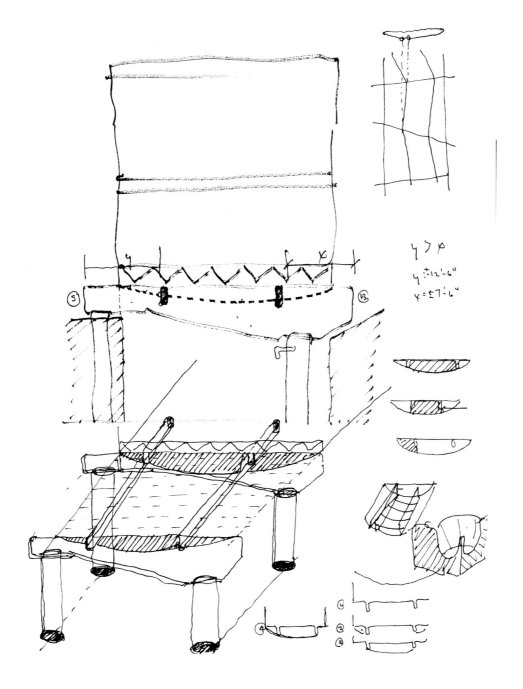

This is a worm's-eye view looking up from below the road at the columns, girders, beams, and soffits. There was the issue of the wall of the block descending vertically, then curving into the soffit. This is a good illustration of the issues of the curved soffit at the edge of the building. If there's a roll-up door on the ground floor, then the soffit above responds as a curve. If not, the soffit is a right angle. There is the truss-joist structure in the ceiling, the big girders, and the "dancing beams" spanning between the girders. And it turns out that in the final framing there is a steel beam on the edge of the block that supports the wall on the edge of the second floor. When in plan the girder crossed that beam at an angle it suggested the possibility that the girder stiffeners would not always be perpendicular to the girder web, as they typically are. In these cases the stiffeners are perpendicular to the steel running at the edge of the soffit. Two angles, welded together, are used to form the intermediate beams that divide the soffit in three.

There is a series of possible soffit sections, ways of understanding the interrelationship between girders, beams, and soffit. In the first example, the soffit turns a right-angle corner and runs horizontally to the little beam, horizontally between beams, and horizontally back to the edge. A second proposition shows the rounded condition at the corner, stopping at the first beam, proceeding on horizontally between beams, and horizontally to the edge. The third option is horizontal on the outsides and curved in the center. These ceiling conditions don't run continuously over the length of each column bay. Each soffit curve varies in length from one girder to the next because the beams that translate the curve aren't parallel to the edge of the block where the curve starts. If you look at the elevation of the intermediate beams, the line of the intersecting curve slopes up or down along the face of these beams.

4.20

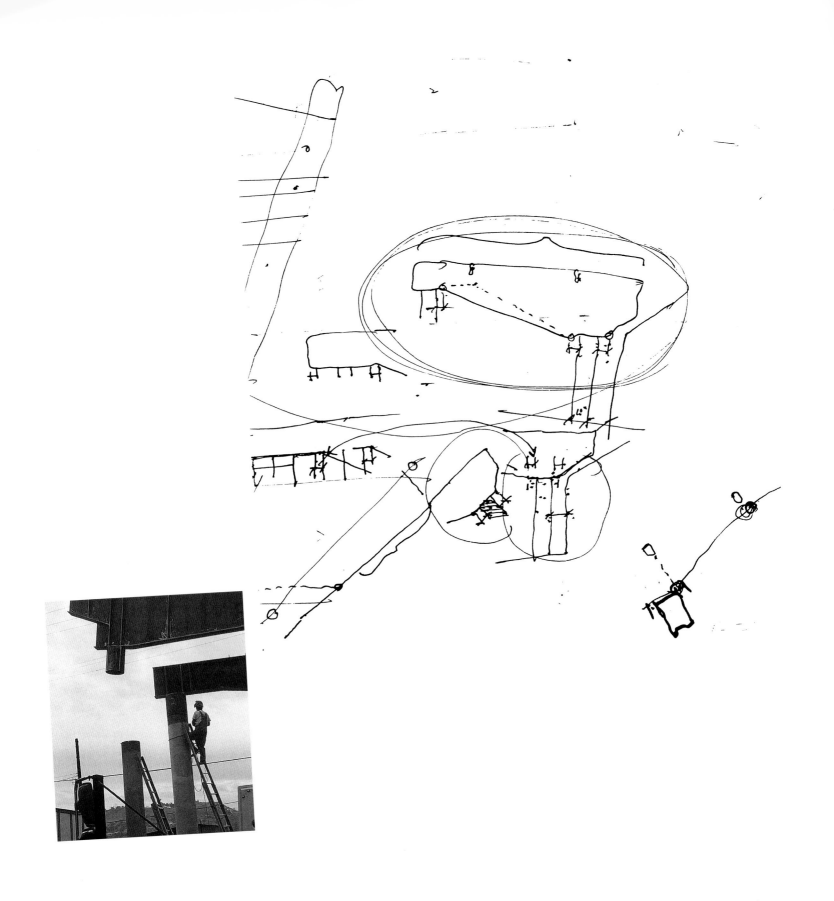

This is more fine-tuning of the dimensional issues—the relationship of columns to girder, and the fixed dimension at the deep end of the girder to accommodate the two different pipe-column diameters. You start to see the location of the intermediate beams relative to the girder face. The beams were initially intended to be structural—and then in the end were not.

The position of the girder's sloped underside and its horizontal aspect were critical. As the girders pivot on the columns at the deep end, rotating to span to the irregularly spaced columns across the road, the horizontal girder dimension had to be sufficiently long to accomodate the difference in span lengths. The flat end of the girder rests on the pipe columns, always in a slightly different location over that horizontal section of the girder. The deep end of the girder always rests on the same column points.

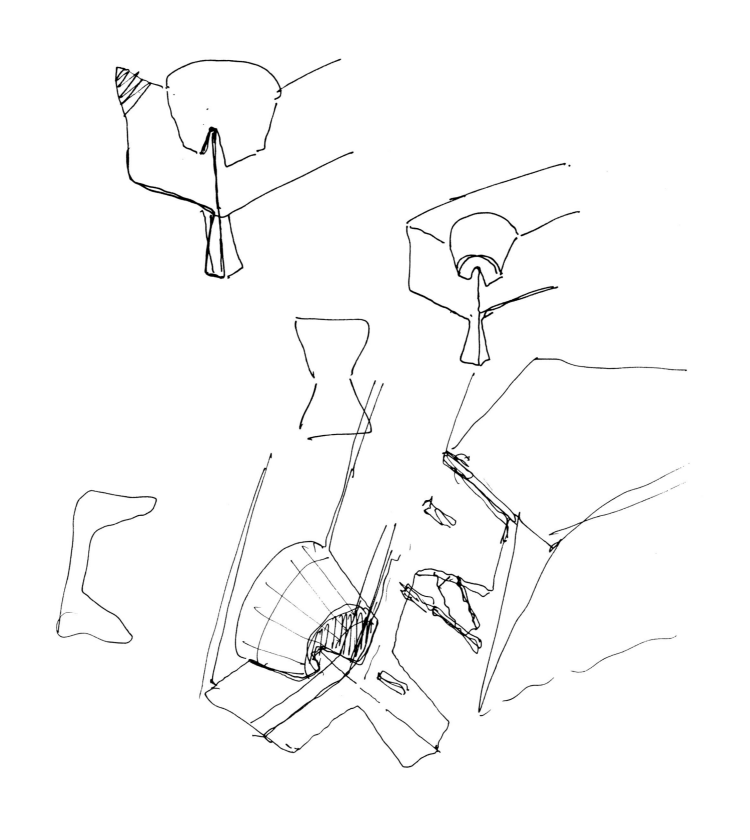

These are all permutations of the entrance stair designs. The partial wall at the street entry and the possible use of a wall instead of columns on the south corner are of particular interest.

In the end the wall appears on the south corner with columns beyond supporting the east edge of the building.

4.22

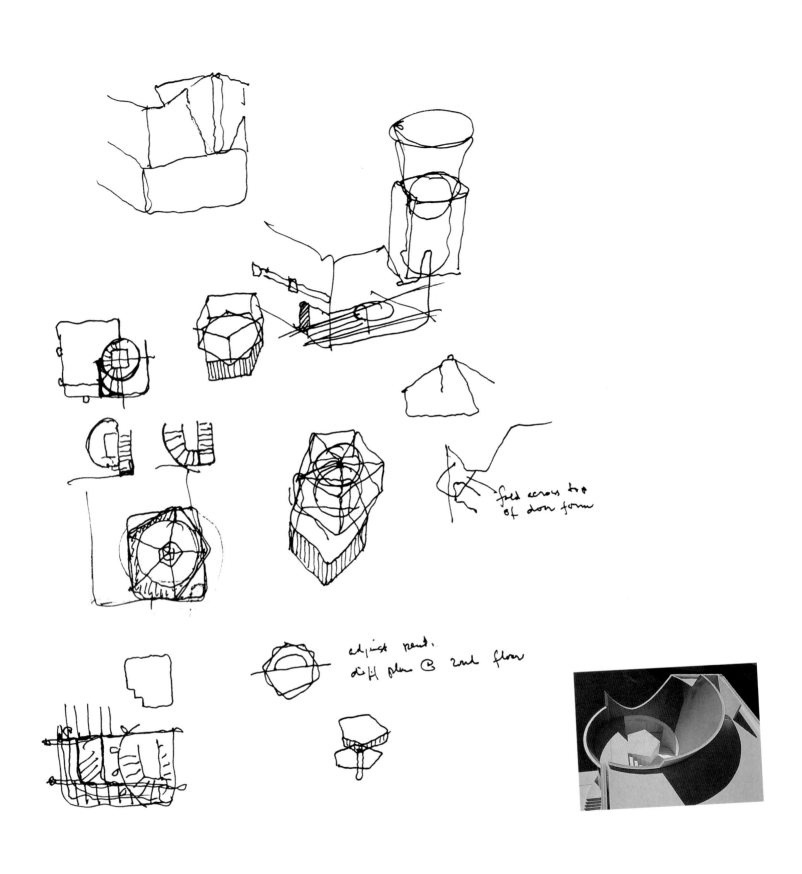

fold across top
of door form

adjust nent.
diff plan @ 2nd floor

The stair form at the corner now includes the corner of the raised block, as well as a cylinder and a five-sided figure which originate at a single center. The shape changed in the final design, but the elements involved are all present here.

The second anomaly, with the pool and the interrelationship of the circle and the two five-sided figures, is also shown. This is drawn two-dimensionally as a section, so a decision regarding the interrelationships of the shapes at one horizontal level doesn't necessarily predict the solution at a different level.

4.23

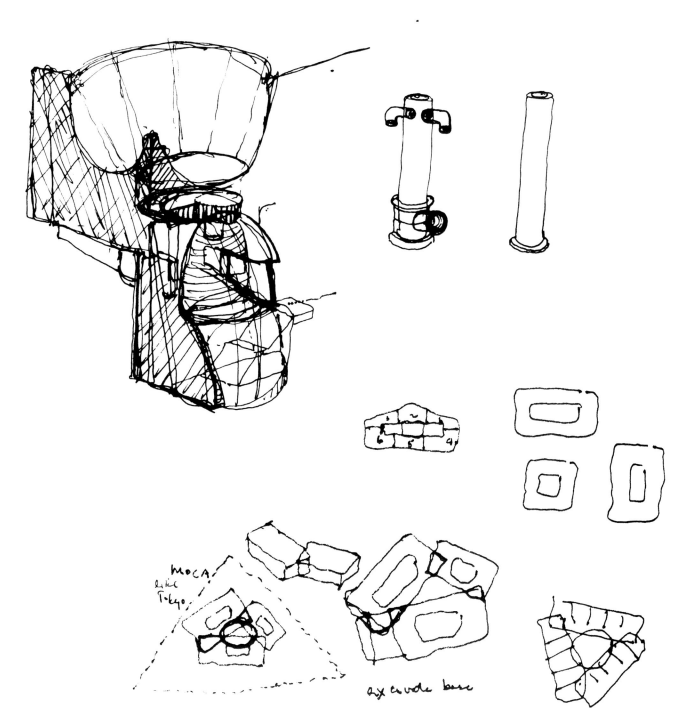

This may have been about a different organizational idea for the site or the strategy for a different project altogether—perhaps Warner Theater.

Originally all the columns in the road were wrapped with corrugated plastic, for protection from trucks and also to distinguish exterior and interior columns. But I dropped all that; it seemed superfluous.

The columns initially had operational distinctions as well, appendages for power and drainage. What you're looking at here are possible differences in the columns. For instance, water is coming out or utilities are coming in. I did a study of the different column types. The columns differ in diameter, in location (inside or outside the building), in finish (corrugated or zinc), and in utilitarian purpose—that is, as structural support and also an additional purpose. That visible operational distinction was rejected in the end in the interest of clarifying the more substantial distinction between the columns. If the building had been built when it was first drawn, in 1988, perhaps those distinctions would have remained.

4.24

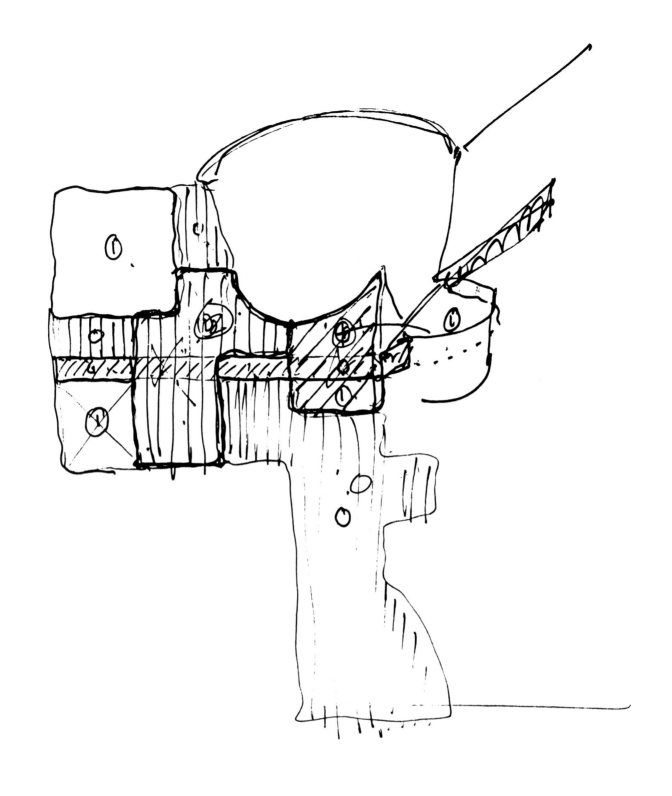

At this point the first anomaly has located itself in the southeast corner of the raised block. There is still an interest in compartmentalizing the elevation, not so much as the block volumes but more as surface divisions, with planes sliding over one another. The anomaly is positioned to extend past the property limits of the building, and the parts that extend past will have to be cut off. Those pieces are removed to suggest the prospect of completion (theoretically) and the realization that is incomplete, set up to be cut away. But the part that is removed returns, as if it were a door swinging out and back. So the missing piece of the cone becomes a cut in the south elevation, the curved window opening. The question is what to do with the missing component. It's gone, but it's back.

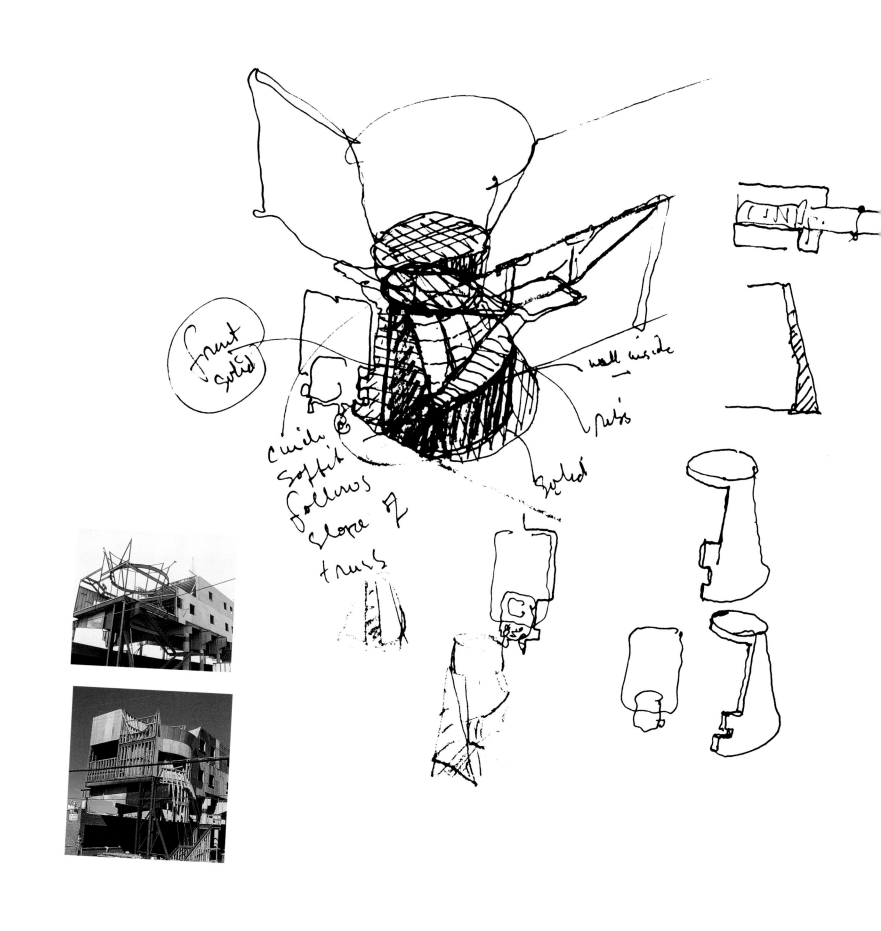

Front solid

wall inside
ribs

curved
soffit
follows
slope of
truss

solid

This is another study of the interrelationship of the cylindrical and conical components at the southeast road entry corner. There's still a strap system in the discussion, and the cone is in the process of being excised from the orthogonal. The hybrid shape on the corner was too large, extending past the corner, and was (eventually) cut off along the right-angle lines of the block.

This is the first sketch of the south window, designed now to corroborate the removed portion of the overhanging cone, which reappears as a puncture in the wall. The intermediate stair landing is exposed in the opening. The first steel-pipe column is buried here in the wall, part of anomaly one at the entrance to the road. An orthogonal plaster shape covers the end of the girder.

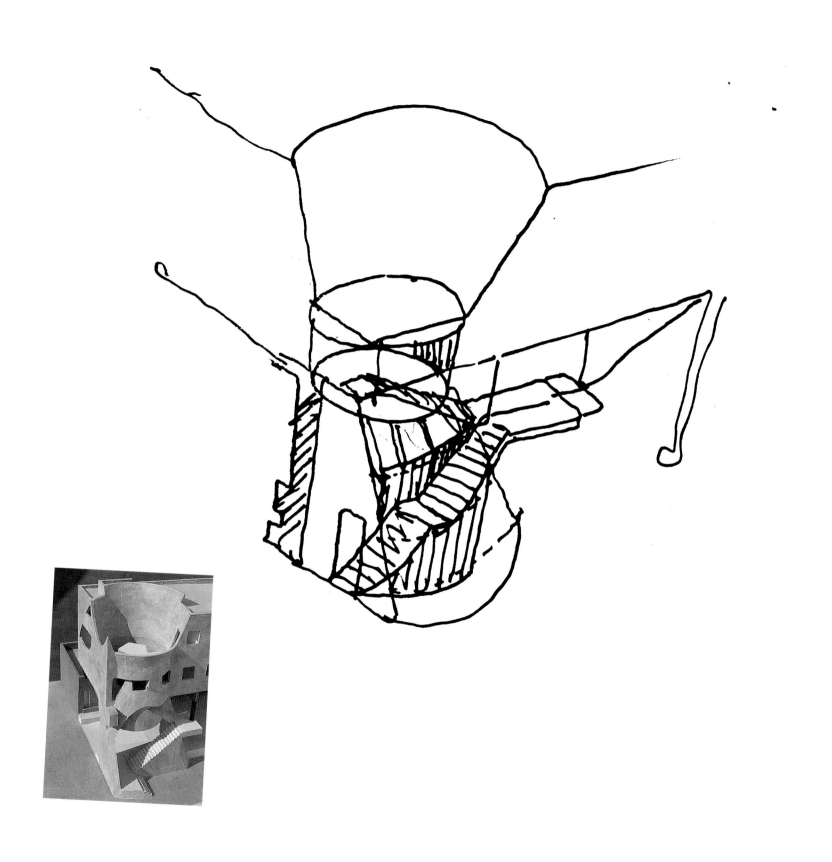

This drawing gets close to representing the final form of the entry anomaly. It's on the southeast corner of the building, the roof deck at the top is hollowed out, the cylinder is present, and the conical base has dropped to intersect the adjoining sloping grade of the driveway next door. The retaining wall that supports the edge of the interior street and separates it from the driveway and the loading dock is there. And the top of the cone is now cut off on the south and east faces of the block.

4.28

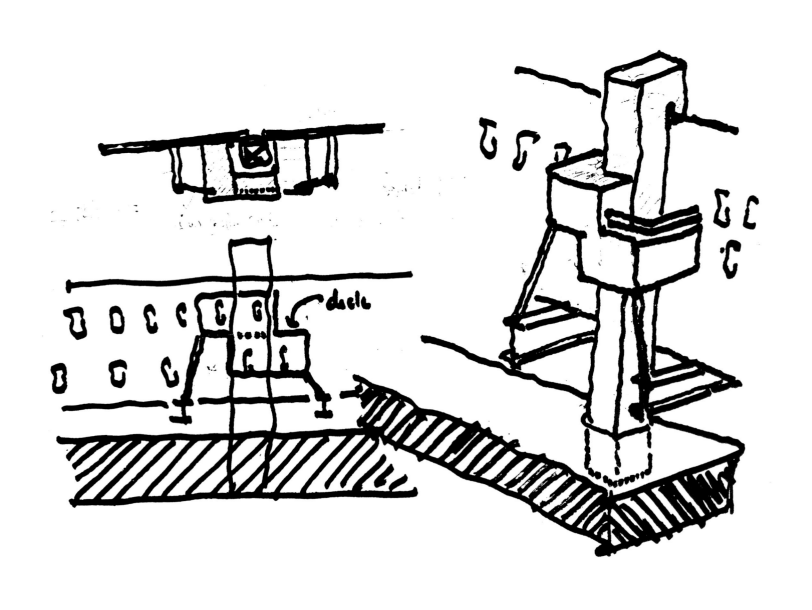

Somebody in my office went to the Los Angeles Building Department to review the building exits and was told that the entry stair in the first anomaly was not a legal exit. We finally won that debate (fortunately), but we had to show them an alternative. This was it. It's a stair stuck on the west wall. You come out on floor two or three and work your way down, exiting on the interior road. It's not a solution; it's just a sketch to show the city another option. Maybe it's an interesting parenthesis.

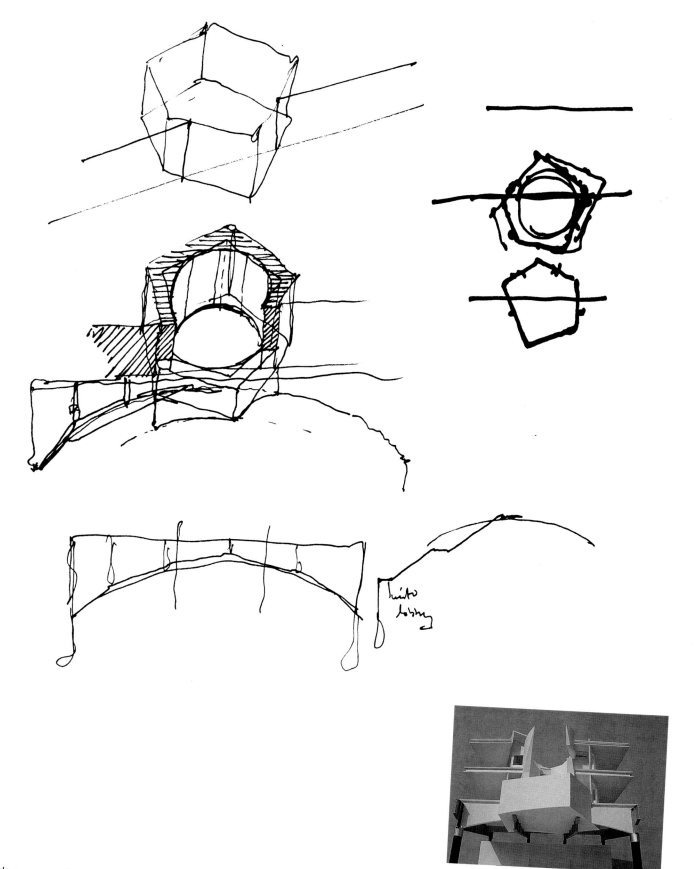

This is the bridge supporting the second anomaly, where two pipe-column supports were removed from the road below so trucks could exit. The anomaly projects west past the plan lines of the block. There is a spanning gesture between the remaining columns, but it's volumetric rather than simply a beam bridging between two columns. The profile of the under-pool area over the truck exit projects past the curved elevation of the bridge. The building extends on the north end over the old sawtooth building below.

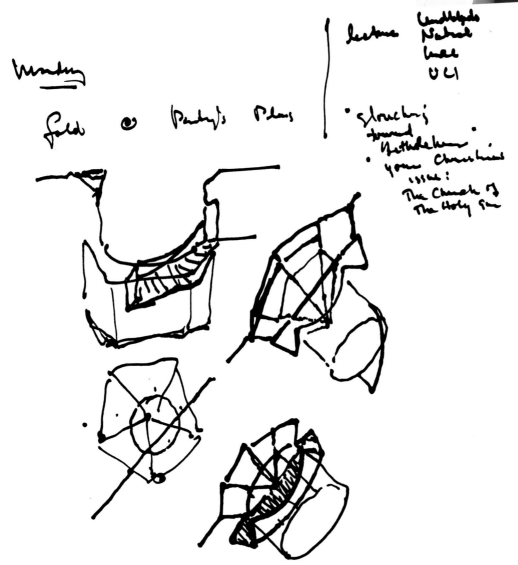

The second anomaly is excised from the block and extends beyond. On the southeast corner of the building, the excess of the first anomaly was cut away beyond the building faces along the property lines. In the area adjacent to the pool, the property line was not the building line, so it was possible to extend the pool deck beyond the plane of the block.

The possible interrelationships between the vertices of the five-sided figures, their centers, and the circle and its center are looked at here. The center of the first or second pentagon could be the center of the circle, but the center of the circle need not be the geometric center of the pentagon(s); both pentagons could have different centers with the circle sharing the center of one; or all three could have different centers.

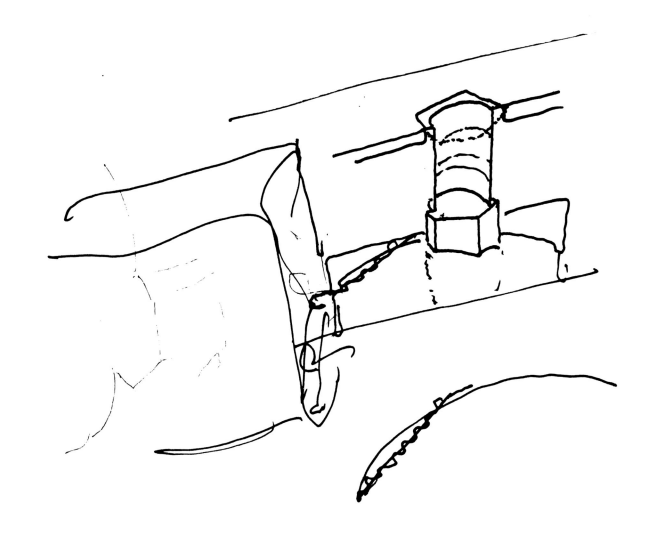

This sketch is very critical in the development of anomaly two. It shows the soffit under the pool area starting to curve in response to the analogue bridge-span curve—columns at either end of the curve in the wall plane, the two columns removed at the girder ends under the pool. Those two girders are now supported by the steel beam buried in the bridge curve wall. Columns out, "bridge" spans the opening, and trucks have clearance to exit the road.

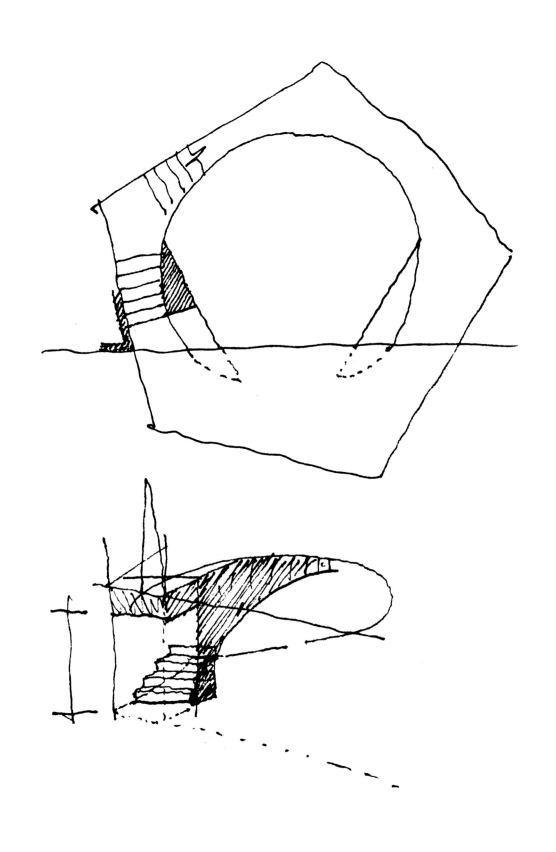

An examination of the pool shape and the fitting of the stair as a residual consequence of adjacent shapes. Also an indication of the second anomaly extending beyond the line of the block, breaking the plane of that otherwise continuous 325-foot-long wall.

4.33

This is of some interest because it describes the interrelationship of the two five-sided volumes that form the perimeter of the pool space in different plan positions and raises the question of the roof form and exposed beam positions and their association with the pool shape on the deck below. The roof folds along the five beam lines. The beams meet at a cylindrical pipe in the air at the pentagon center. The sloping sides of the pool originate on the deck at the pentagon's vertices and slope down to a five-sided plate drain at the bottom of the pool. The sides of the pool slope up from the drain as the folded faces of the metal roof slope down from above.

4.34

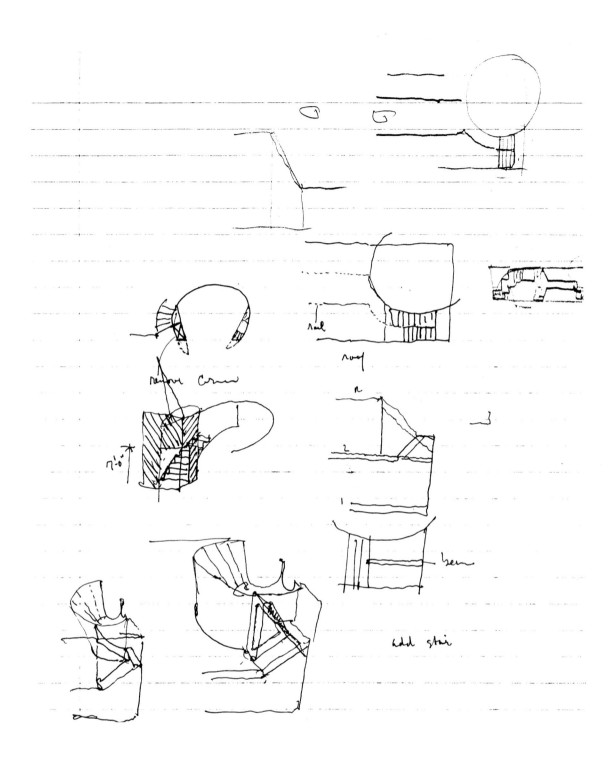

This is a fairly accurate rendition of the circular edge of the pool in anomaly two, the interrelationship of the five-sided figure and the circle, and the stair from the roof to the deck interpolating between the two. Various ways of positioning the stair adjacent to that curved plan form are studied.

There is also the soffit/ceiling of the road as the underside of the pool. What happens to the shape of the ceiling is the opposite of the concave pool form. The ceiling under the pool reverses the pool section shape with respect to the road. It's convex. And it extends the curving elevation of the long span bridge at the truck egress point (directly under the pool). That curve continues inside the block to form a five-sided convex ceiling, which is not shown here.

4.35

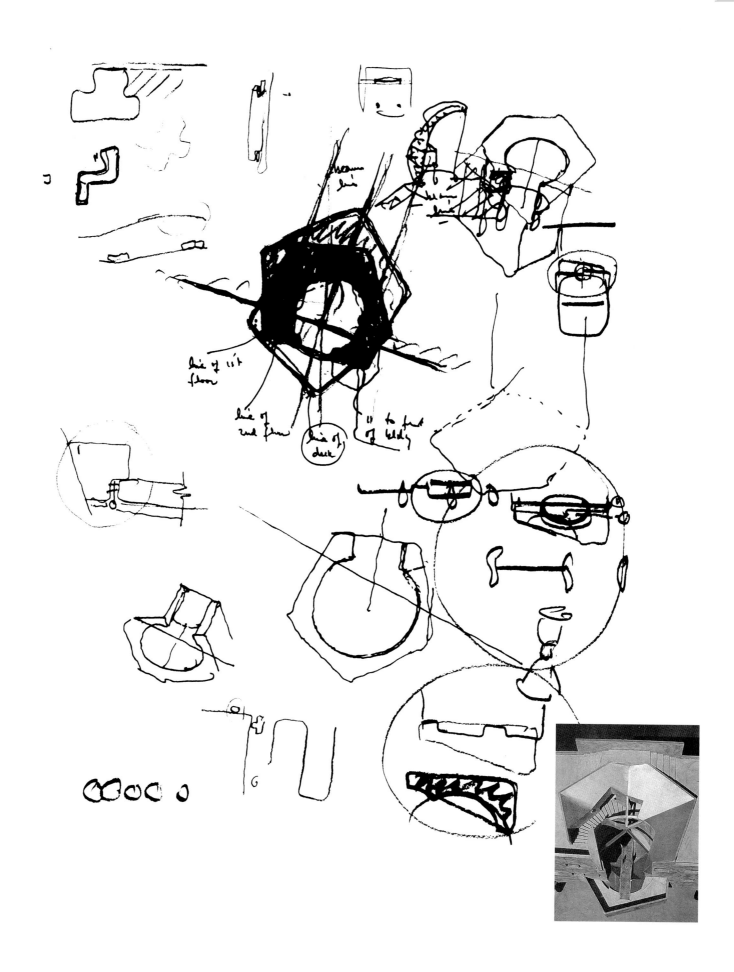

Another study of the plan and section relationship between the two five-sided figures and the cylinder in the second anomaly. All those separate geometric priorities are now integrated to form the space. The stair works its way up around the perimeter, looking into the space that takes you from the pool area to the third floor and then to the roof.

There's also a different profile for the girder, sketched here, which never went very far.

## *Little Rock*
# EXCELSIOR HOTEL

**Dear Guest,**
    In order to better serve you, if we can refer your phone calls while you are out of the room, please allow us.

Between the hours of _____ and _____, I will be at

La Petite Roche ☐     Pinnacle Lounge ☐

Apple Blossom ☐     Room No. _____ ☐

Edgewater Bar ☐     _____ ☐

Name: _____ Room # _____

**Notes**

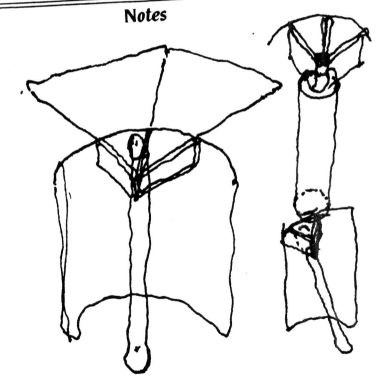

This is a study of the edge of the roof at the second anomaly: the relation of the radical beams to the roof shape and the issue of catching the water somehow on the tops of the beams and carrying or dropping it through a pipe to the pool below.

4.37

*Little Rock*

# EXCELSIOR HOTEL

**Dear Guest,**
   In order to better serve you, if we can refer your phone calls while you are out of the room, please allow us.

Between the hours of _____

_____ **and**

_____, **I will be at**

**La Petite Roche**          Pinnacle Lounge          ☐

**Apple Blossom**      ☐   Room No. _____      ☐

**Edgewater Bar**     ☐   _____   ☐

Name: _____ Room # _____

                                             Notes

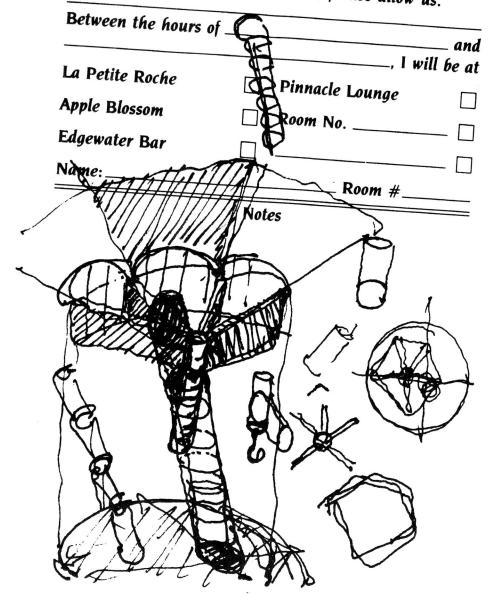

Here the edge of the roof is conceived as a sequence of curves, which finally became a sequence of straight lines. And another study of the intersection of the beam lines. Those beams also appear on the inside of the building. They're exposed outside over the bridge, disappear under the sloping roof structure, and emerge as an exposed interior structure surrounding the second anomaly on the third floor.

Again the dropping water and the question of how the water is transported to the pool, the order of the double pentagon centers, a circle with its center, and two five-sided figures with their centers and how they interconnect.

Originally called the Hook (because of its enclosed courtyard), Samitaur 2 was first designed in 1991.

The Los Angeles mayor's office began to show interest in the project site during the construction of Phase 1 in 1995. They called my office and asked if I could add a fourth floor to the block. I couldn't. We got into a discussion about the area—the departed manufacturing uses; the positive psychological value of the project for a deteriorating, riot-devastated area; and finally, the uselessness of the current height, parking, setback, and use limits. They suggested a study for a Phase 2 building that would substantially exceed the height limit. There are three versions of Phase 2: the first was the Hook, a courtyard that stayed within the original forty-five-foot height limit and followed the existing zoning rules (1991). The second, after the phone call from the mayor's office, included a tower 126 feet high (1995), and the third, current version, kept the tower but omitted the courtyard in order to preserve a substantial portion of an existing sawtooth building (1997). The height limits and other zoning requirements for preserving an industrial zone didn't make much sense since industry had long since departed. The mayor's office understood that clearly and helped to make a new conception plausible.

4.39

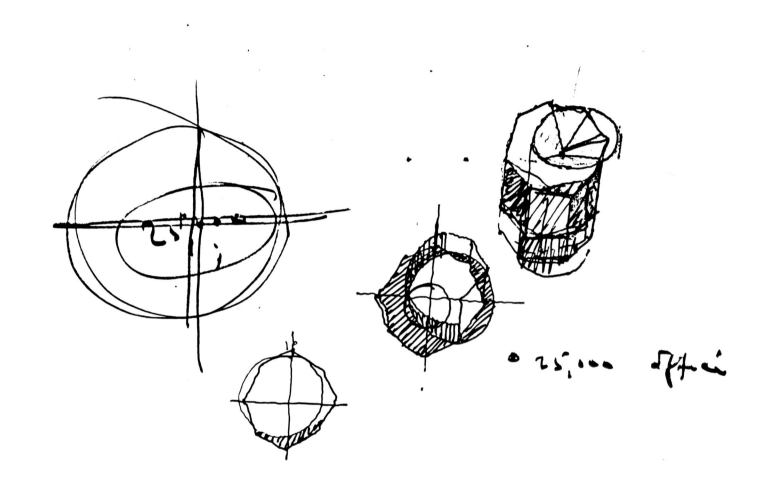

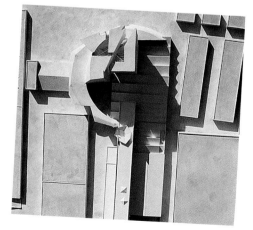

The Hook begins, providing an introverted space on the site and extending the spatial language of anomaly two where the Hook was to originate.

4.40

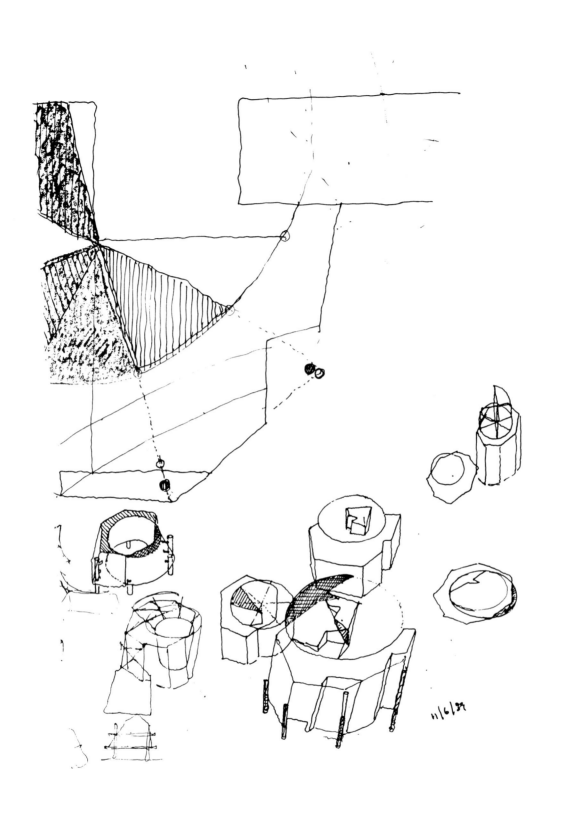

This is a study of the interrelationship of the cylindrical and the six-sided pieces of the Hook—how they fit together in section, how they work in plan. The block extends into the court. Here we see how it will work in section with the possibility of the frame outside the shape, the shape inside the frame, or some of both. It looks at how the shape of the building relates to what supports the shape and whether the structural system defers to the shape or has its own obligations that might, in some cases, project outside. We're actually still considering these options, although the object is significantly different.

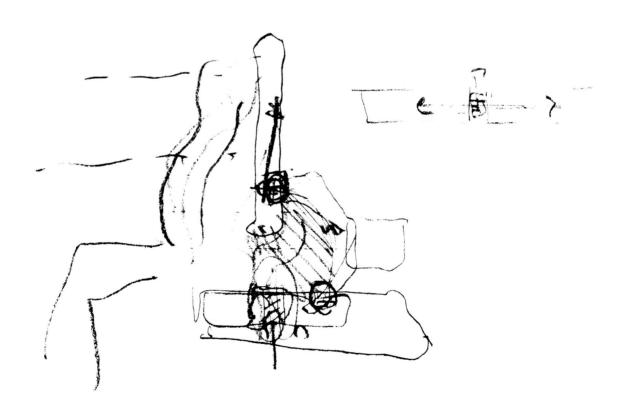

Another drawing of the coagulation of volumes that results in the Hook.

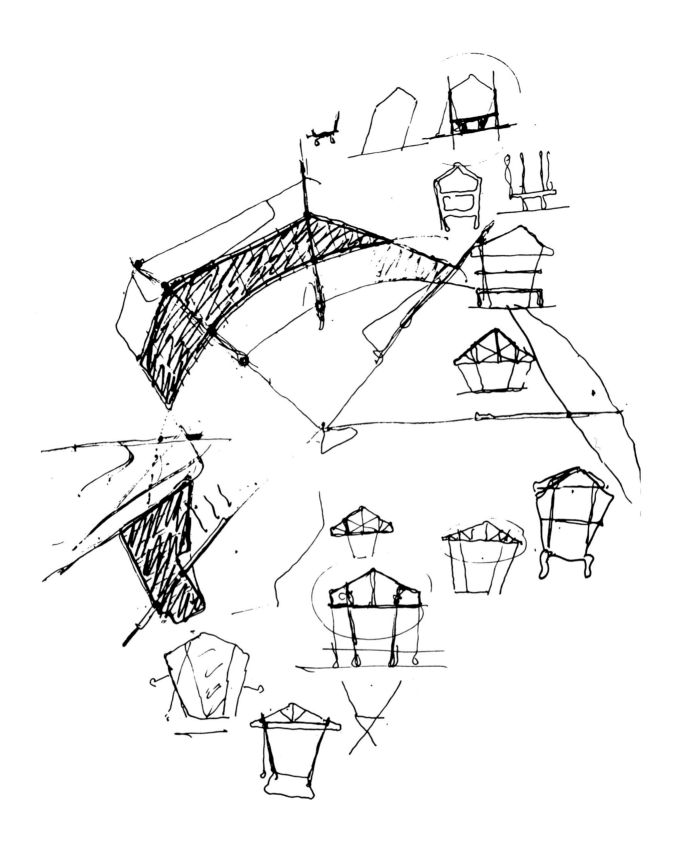

An investigation of centers and structure—centers at different levels, centers for different figures, structure in the frame, structure out of the frame, structure as contingent on the antecedent building, structure as contingent on the new building, structure as contingent on the two opposing pieces in the new building.

4.43     There is an exploration here of both concentric and radial systems of support structure, particularly in section.

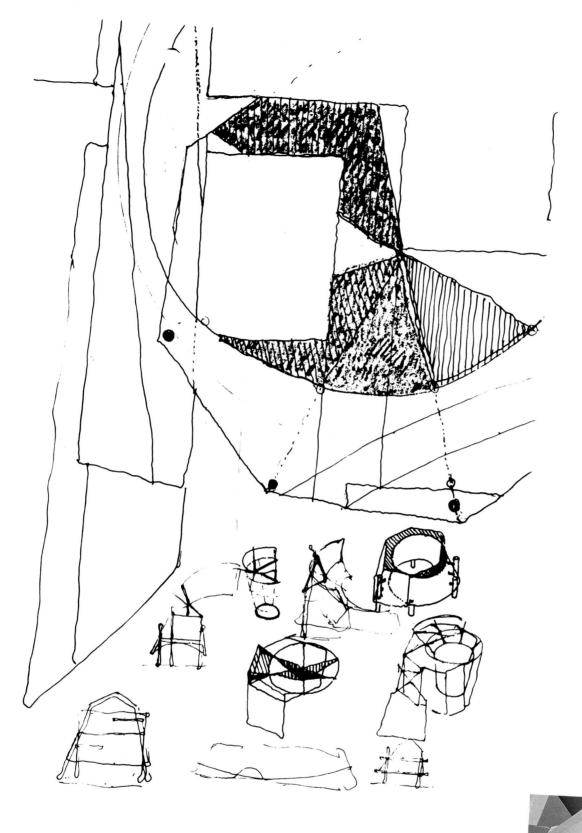

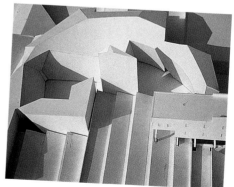

There was another component of Phase 2—the building along Jefferson Boulevard. The straight line on the left adjoins Jefferson. This anticipates the interrelationship of the parts that make up the courtyard building with the shape of the streetfront building.

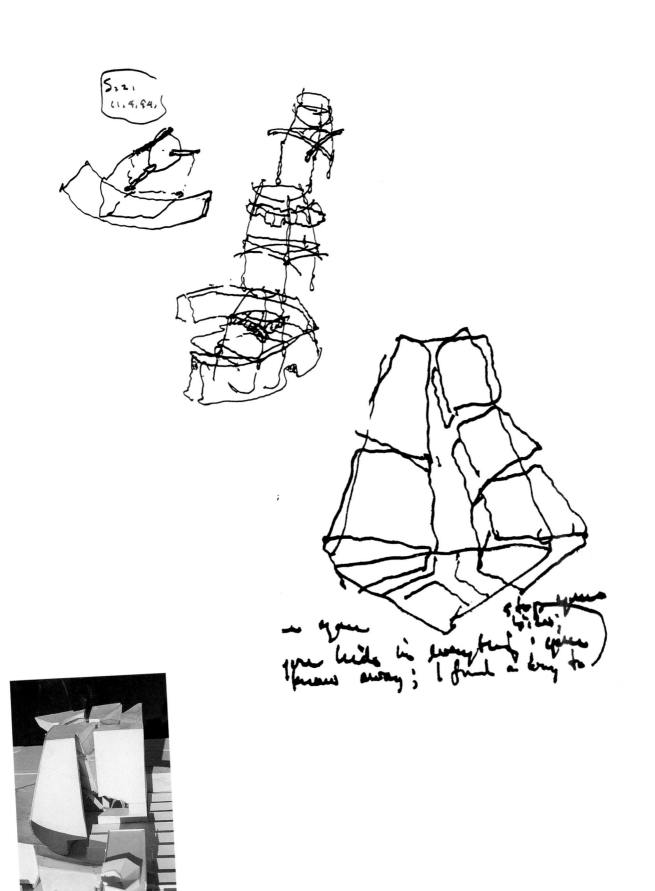

This is the second version of the second phase of Samitaur 2 (1995). The courtyard is preserved in concept and a tower is assembled in pieces over the courtyard. The discrete pieces preserve the view to the city from the Samitaur 1 boardroom, which looks north between the elements. By the time elevators and exit stairs were positioned the pieces were difficult to inhabit. It didn't work functionally, though it was of interest spatially.

4.45

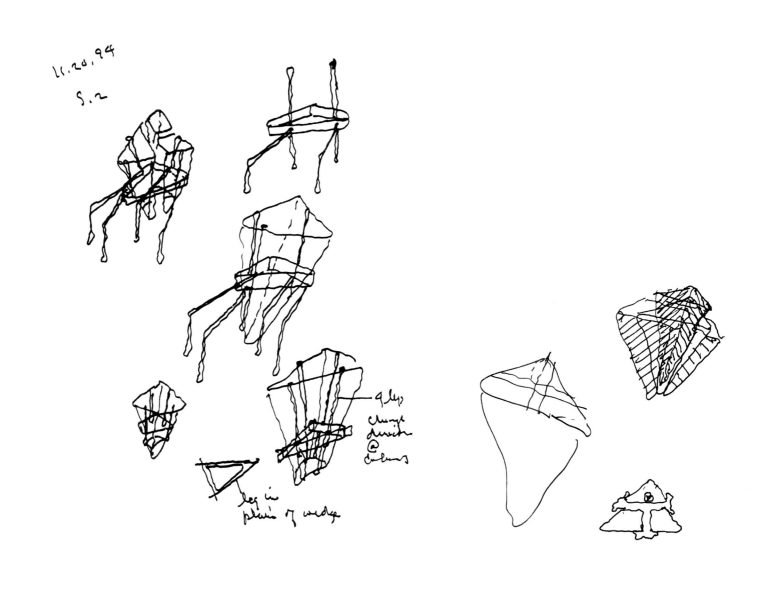

Another study of a possible structural system for holding the building parts and also the enclosures that separate circulation from office space. The reaching of these column legs and their points of origin can be traced back to the order of the Hook— the six-sided figure, the circular figure, the geometric regulations of each, and the regulations invented from the hybridization of the two shapes.

Originally the shape was three-sided, then it was subdivided by a horizontal movement system. This scheme was replaced by a different tower and a different plan organization on the ground, which is the current working version of Samitaur 2. Then we moved on to Samitaur 3—the high-rises on the next site.

4.46

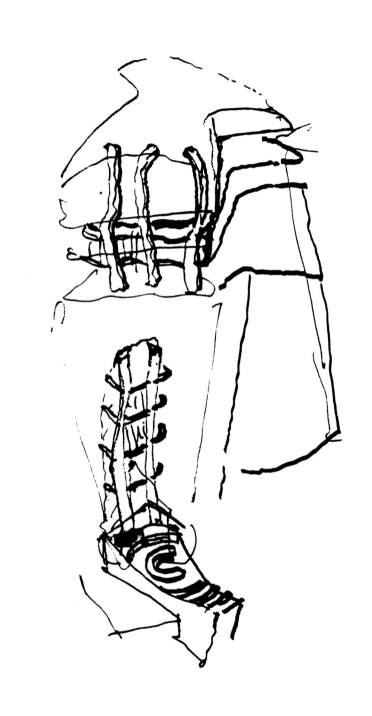

Detail of the knitted-steel elevator core that anticipates the penthouse structure. Also, the beginnings of an open-air

4.47    theater/gathering space—once the courtyard of the Hook.

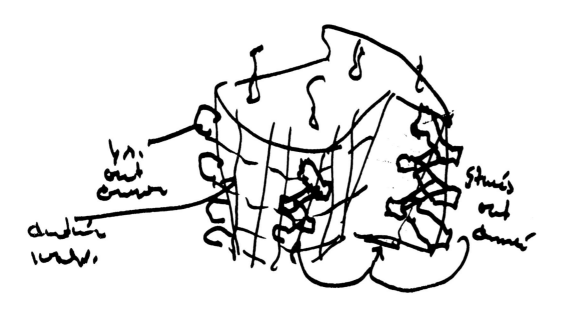

Fire exit stair and the beginning of the glass wall enclosing the tower on the north end.

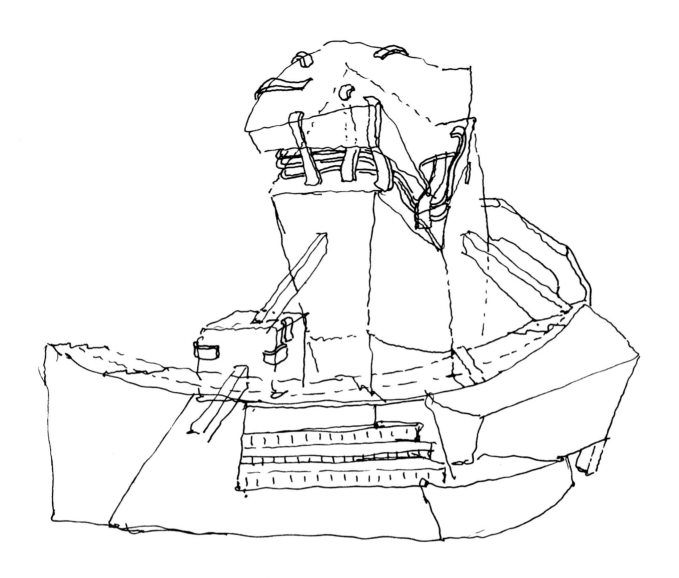

slots:
stairs up and
down to
bleachers

model
- Hydra of roof
- pin walls @
  penthouse
- soffit @ cut roof
- 2nd floor
- stair towers @
  corners
- stairs @ high rise

Preliminary sketch of Samitaur 2, version three, showing roof deck, penthouse, and conference block. The residual shape of
the Hook remains at the base.

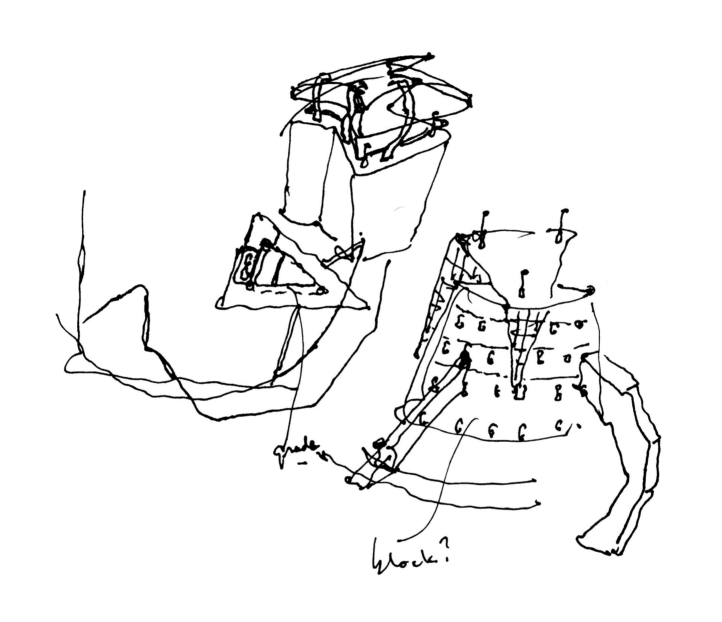

grade

block?

Study of the tower west wall, the exit-stair supports, and the penthouse structure.

# 5

# INSIDE <small>OF THE</small> INSIDE

From where I sit today, I can look back in time over both long and short distances and review any number of prognostications from any number of extraordinary people: how the world works; how history moves; what motivates men and women. None of these paradigms—however incisive, intriguing, or erudite—seem adequate or complete, notwithstanding the predictable enthusiasm of the prognosticators who often incline toward the proposition that they have now explained everything. Always the explanation derives from a particular vantage point: aesthetic, historic, economic, psychological. What I'm always looking for is a way both to explain and to free myself from the limits of the explanation. I'm arguing for developing an instinct for synthesizing, for understanding, but simultaneously knowing that what you synthesize will ultimately break down, arrive at a limit, need to become other than the synthesis. You don't ever complete the process. You never arrive at a final conclusion. The process never stops with me. So I'm always looking for what is still, and still moving.

Reading a biography of Mark Rothko,[1] I recognized in the artist a quality I can generalize as a behavioral component of what this century has called the avant-garde. That pattern mixes a moral imperative and a generous portion of personal vanity. What Rothko wanted to do was to find a vantage point, a way of seeing and understanding that originated with him, that he could attribute to himself, that didn't precede him. There is a quote from Umberto Eco's novel *Foucault's Pendulum*[2] that describes this: "What I have, I have given."

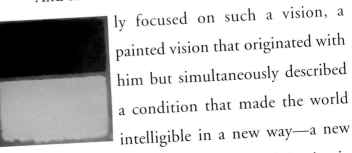

And so Rothko,[3] it seems to me, was singularly focused on such a vision, a painted vision that originated with him but simultaneously described a condition that made the world intelligible in a new way—a new world. A generically applicable insight, originating in a single individual, discovered by a single individual, or, perhaps better, invented by a single individual, so we see differently—how we see (and understand) what we see has changed.

1. See 3.26–27.
2. See 3.12.
3. Mark Rothko, #18, 1963.

In Rothko's later paintings, what matters to me and, I think, what ratified my position, was that I could see something I would describe as moving toward orthogonal, right angle, rectangular. Something you can write an equation for—almost. You know it. You've seen it. It's in the world's ethos. It comes to your head as an antecedent form of constructed life, or from the Euclidian chapter of your education.[4] But something else is going on in the paintings—a movement toward the more ethereal. You see it on the edge of the shape, you see it in the ambiguous color that defies a simple naming. You can't quite say what the painted shape is; but it's not so nebulous that it could be anything. It has the once orthogonal reading. But now it's in between the right angle and the not–right angle, between what might be remembered and what is not quite formed. (I'm associating the idea of memory with the recall of standard models, of archetypes collectively understood, whereas the making of the future, the not-yet-formed, is necessarily a private act.)

In Rothko's painting there is an appeal to the recollected, to the once known—the ex-orthogonal. There is also an opposing instinct away from what we've met toward something we can't recognize. The content of the painting is moving in both directions simultaneously, while, of course, the work remains literally a painting—paint dried, empirically still. So it's pulling conceptually and standing still physically. That poignant expression of tension is Rothko's invention: how to express the tension between something one recognizes and something less clear. What Rothko did was to make both prospects intelligible simultaneously—a cerebral dialectic **delivered in paint that I'm interested in reconstituting architecturally.**

But beyond, or over and above this intellectual tension is the possibility of a transcendent resolution of the dialectical conflict. The dialectic is, or can be, subsumed by the poetry. That is, the work can contain the dialectic intellectually, and overcome it lyrically. I call this the dialectical lyric.[5] **The lyric**

---

4. See 3.14. See also 3.27 and 3.28.     5. See 1.4.

doesn't deny the cerebral argument. It only says that there is the prospect of a spatial experience that transcends the intellectual plane of the dialectical argument if the dialectic is poignantly communicated. That is, the poignancy of the dialectic affords its overcoming. Gnosis is transcendent knowledge, not empirical knowledge. The conception of Gnosis originates in a religious context as a knowledge that gains from, then supersedes, the stress of history. Gnostic architecture builds transcendent space—in time, out of time.[6]

As I attempt to define the lyric as a space form, **the lyric is perfectible, but the conflict can never be resolved on an intellectual plane.** Eliot's famous phrase from *Four Quartets,*[6] "the still point of the turning world," is certainly about a pivot point of tension, although it may also be about the overcoming of that tension. It can't go further. No additions. No subtractions. But the dialectical quality of the intellectual argument remains taut. **If architecture is a tangible exorcising of living and the issues of living, then architecture is in tension too.** Exorcising stress might transcend the stress if the exorcising is powerful enough **to transcend the intellectual dialectic and**

become Gnosis.

The lyric suggests an overcoming—the prospect that the world could become something other than it is something other than what we know and recall; that the categories, the nomenclature, the labels, the configurations that constitute our experiences are mutable, changeable, and might bring us to something we don't yet know and can't anticipate: C. S. Lewis's Narnia, through the wardrobe door, for example. Not everybody could go through Lewis's door, however. Or as Matthew put it, we see the world only "through a glass darkly." What we think we know is both moving and unclear. Turner's paintings[7] communicate a similar sensibility: the fog ascends, descends, and a complicated, incomplete, evolving view is all that's possible. I want to call this the **provisional paradigm,** provisional because, contrary to other *creative* models, this one sees itself as only a temporary way to proceed, not a fixed law. The provisional paradigm foresees its own demise and replacement.

As with Rothko's shapes, so with his colors: the color of the PS Office Building is a comparable example, as is the color of the Box, and the color of the Lawson/Westen House.[8] In each case color

7. See 3.32.
8. Exterior surfaces (opposite) Top to bottom: the PS Office Building, the Box, and the Lawson/Westen House. See also 1.9.

6. Cover of Eliot's Four Quartets.

selection was a long exploration. One fundamental intention was to arrive at a surface color one couldn't recognize or name. **And this effort to create outside the limits of memory is the criterion for the color at Samitaur, as well as for the nature of the spatial experience,** which has the higher priority. The aspiration is always that the building be both known

and unknown—that it suggest the world is as it is, and that it suggest the world might be something other than it is.

Some insist that meaning comes only from progress, from going forward, whatever exactly that is. What I'm proposing is that the truth is the tension between the past and future possibilities,[9] not an allegiance to either one. Those oppositions should read in the architecture. If the architectural expression is sufficiently powerful, its poetry provides the experiential way out of the intellectual dilemma that is manifest in the representation of the tension. The lyric is the only way out. Choosing only the recollection or the forward won't work. Such a choice avoids

what is intrinsic to the experience of living. Don't believe the psychologist who councils getting rid of stress. That psychologist has it backward: look for the stress to relieve stress and then perhaps for a moment, (in space) you're the Gnostic who overcomes a moment in time. Poetry (historically) jumps over history lyrically.

It's important to understand that the artist makes an intricate experience available. The Rothko paintings have a particular meaning for me at a particular time. The exegesis that I am offering is useful to me now; it confirms some of my feelings about the creation of space, about shape, about color, and about the origin of original architecture.

The process of design has to be personal. I'm not sure that the word *design* is useful if it simply signifies the resolution of a list of problems. Design is the process through which the architect builds himself, finding a way to extrapolate, piece by piece, what she learns to the form language of space making. This makes architecture both a private, personal process and, assuming what one learns is applicable to others, a generic undertaking—when you construct yourself you construct everyone else. That conception is also applicable to painting. In that sense Rothko[10] painted himself. Biblically, he floated the paint on the water. Some people let it sink; some  drank it up, and recognized the insight. I don't think the message ever comes back exactly the way the artist sends it out. And I'm not even sure that the person who sends it out knows explicitly what message is sent. The exchange is always inexact, always requiring an interpretation by the receiver.

There are two extreme positions regarding what one learns—antecedent influences. One chooses not to recognize them: "Everything I do originates with me. Nobody ever assisted. I do it all alone." The other does: "Somehow references arrive and coagulate in my head at various points in my life, informing and ratifying the efforts of that moment." Sometimes a new reference can reinform an old project.

Some students once asked me if I became acquainted with Henry Moore's *Helmet*[11] prior to

 using it as an aesthetic analogue for the Box.[12] The project preceded my knowing *Helmet*. When I became acquainted with the sculpture, I could see a certain relationship between the two, so I could talk about the Box and *Helmet* together, not as if one were the impetus for or inspired the other, but as if the predilections of the pieces were shared.

Everyone who does what I do uses himself or herself as the raw material from which concepts emerge. You start by being disconnected—an infinite number of pieces. Ultimately you discover points of contact between the pieces, yours and others'. Brueghel's painting *Children's Games*[13] is illustrative. My interest in the painting really isn't about the content or subject. The painting is extremely  complicated. All kinds of adventures are occurring at once. The circumstances of the painting are a very good indication of our problem: how to intervene in infinitely complex circumstances and say what they might mean. Whether you start geographically and sequentially from this corner of the painting and work this way, or

10. *Mark Rothko*, White Band, *1954.*
11. *See 1.4–5. See also 1.8, and 3.15.*
12. *EOM, the Box, 1994.*
13. *Brueghel,* Children's Games, *1568.*

that corner and work that way, or thematically, from the hoops to the barrels, the examination begins to suggest the possibility that **there is no intrinsic paradigm. Only extrinsic models.** Only the patterns you or I impose.

In order to develop an architectural point of view (and an exegesis for the painting), what I had to do (in retrospect, instinctively, not methodically) was to jump in somewhere, into the painting, and say, "Okay, of all of these prospects, *this* is what it is, *this* is where it goes." You can go back hundreds of years, thousands of years, and find cultures defining themselves, imposing on themselves exegesis criteria like what I'm imposing on the painting. Whether it's the king, the magician, or the priest; whether it's done by a monk in Tibet, a council in St. Peter's, or a scientist at Princeton, **they produce a paradigm of the world the way they want it, feel it, need the world to be understood. Then they ask their invention what the world is like. A very fascinating and somewhat disingenuous game.**

**A paradigm is a prayer for order.** Newton made a model. He didn't know electromagnetism. Marx made a model. He omitted the resilient middle

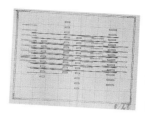
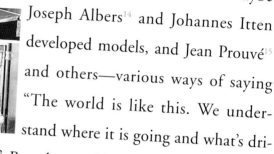

class. Freud made a model. He left out Jung. Darwin made a model. He forgot the cliffs of Chile. Maybe Joseph Albers[14] and Johannes Itten developed models, and Jean Prouvé[15] and others—various ways of saying "The world is like this. We understand where it is going and what's driving it." But the world never quite goes there.

Every paradigm has aesthetic manifestations—objects ordered in space. Take the Brueghel painting again, impossibly dense. What's going on? **What underlies that density, I think, is a prayer for coherence. The prayer asks that there be a straight line through all these myriad mysteries that could make this web of apparently contradictory senses, feelings, and up-and-down events legible and intelligible.** Build some colossal structure for the priests in Angkor Wat;[16] etch stupendous drawings into the plains of Nazca;[17] congregate in Rome and hammer out a church, and attribute its direction to people who would be astonished to see what has been attributed to them. Such a model

14. *Joseph Albers,* Homage to the Square, *1965.*
15. *Jean Prouvé, detail of table.* See 3.9 (Chaplin).
16. *See 3.4–5.*
17. *See 3.21. See also 1.2.*

allows the culture to account for its origin, its history, its present, to anticipate the future, to answer its prayer.

In the search for paradigms, it seems to me that the most durable laws involve human behavior—what you'll do to me, and what I'll do to you, and why. Those patterns seem the most predictable, though not free of exceptions. The least durable models are the so-called scientific laws that, at first glance, seem to the empirical culture to be the most durable, notwithstanding the fact that the scientific priesthood periodically decrees and updates and sometimes inverts the doctrine.

If you were an animated version of one of Brueghel's skeletons, trying to understand the whole painting and knowing the limits of what you could see, and the peculiar vantage point that you held within the frame, would it be conceivable to say that there was anything like a coherent representation of this event, any abstract model to which the apparent complexity could appeal for explanation? Or would it remain only as the perception that resides in the head of each skeleton? I think both the abstract suprapersonal and the unique, peculiarly personal are operative.

By analogy it's like the difference between the drafts of this book and the completed version. Depending on how much of each draft becomes part of the final book, a reader examining the drafts might get a somewhat different sense of the final meaning. One of the critical issues in architecture is to communicate a sense or sustain the prospect that a building (or a life) could go many places. Finally I say "I'll do this, and I won't do that." That's difficult for me, and my guess is, in a very fundamental way, it's difficult for everyone making choices. But I can be a very tough character and say "Okay, I went down Broadway and skipped Amsterdam." I can say that, but in my head, the Amsterdam possibility still exists, and therefore it has a psychological reality. It sticks around. I have a stake in making that hypothetical prospect architecturally tangible.

There are two images I use in my lectures. One shows the assembly of several Pythagorean triangles: right angles, sides, hypotenuses.[18] The counter-image is a Rembrandt painting, *The Sacrifice of Isaac.*[19] Here's the Pythagorean law—understanding based on quantity, measure, proportion. Humanity's invention. Something we have come to feel is incontrovertible. So I want to indicate that Pythagorean law is only law in a certain world that

18. See 3.25.
19. Rembrandt, Sacrifice of Isaac, 1634 (opposite).
See also 3.25 (Pythagoras).

has clear limits. The contrary law happens in a different frame of reference. What force, what law, what way of understanding, what fear would compel Abraham to take his son to the mountain in Moriah and execute him? I don't  know how to represent that law. I can't utter it, but I feel it exists. And maybe that's sufficient to undermine the other side—the logical, empirical side. Pythagoras could be a tiny section of Abraham's knife blade. In other words, **the rules we "know" to be intrinsically so are, perhaps, only extrinsic: our inventions; our impositions**. Pythagoras thought his triangle was evidence of the world's underlying logic. And then Rembrandt arrives with the Abrahamic sensibility that makes Pythagoras a logical part of an alogical whole.

The question is not whether Pythagoras's hypothesis[20] or, by extension, Descartes's grid[21] have any pragmatic applicability. I'm not saying we ought to terminate the triangle and grid, put them away as a manifestation of a narrow kind of thinking—but we ought to understand them for what they are. I think most of the time we don't; we treat the grid as

a conceptual essence. **Perhaps it's just a surface manifestation of the need to manage legibly.**

**If you look beneath the form, or the form language, or the expressed method, you will always locate the necessity to find and replicate a consistent pattern**. But the pattern itself is not found. You can see the attempt to find the law or pattern in Darwin,[22] or Vico, or Marx, or Brueghel, or Rothko. What is the pattern beneath the appearance? As I keep digging, I'm not sure I won't always come back to another appearance. And that appearance is the pattern underneath the pattern. You never reach the bottom.

6.19  A comparison of the skeletons of the gorilla (a) and man (b). The pelvic region of the gorilla is very long and tilts forward, whereas that of man is short and upright. In the gorilla, the vertebral column does not have the typical S-curve found in man, the shoulder girdle is more massive than a man's, the arms are longer than the legs, the feet have no pronounced arches, and the head hangs forward.

I would like to try to introduce a force field of contradictory ideas and sensibilities, developed spatially in the most expressive ways, that would both exploit these ideas in the most extreme ways and suggest their limitations.

My conceptual premise is that the truth of any argument, architecture not excepted, is the tension that is *found* between a proposition and its

20. See 3.25.
21. See 3.20 (Moon Map).
22. The Evolution of Man. See also 3.3 (Altamira).

dialectical opposite. My objective wouldn't be to say that one position is right and the other wrong. Rather, I want to say that in order to understand, you have to position yourself in the center and at the edge at the same time.

Many cultures have posited that the ideal, the ultimate state, the superior truth is behind them in time. It exists as a durable principle, to be recalled, not to be advanced or improved upon with time. So truth would be behind you, like the memory of Euclid in Rothko.

In the dominant Western scientific perspective of the last several hundred years, the truth we have posited seems always to be in front of us—the next invention, the next insight, the next discovery, the next philosophical synthesis. It's called progress. I would like to advocate a way of making architecture that mandates the truth both behind and in front of you—recollecting forward.

My intention is to try, at least provisionally, to arrive at a conceptual symmetry. I want to place these oppositions as precisely as possible into what is built. And then finally, if what is built communicates the dialectic, or the conflict, or the tension, as in the Rothko example, then I want the object to transcend the dialectic poetically, to reconcile emotionally what should remain tense intellectually. The dialectic sustains itself at an intellectual level but is subsumed by the poetry of the architecture.

One doesn't have to align oneself with the New Urbanists or the Deconstructivists or the Neo-minimalists. Those allegiances, simply put, miss the point that there are always powerful contradictory points. **This Gnostic architecture idea comes not**  **from the early Christians (the term precedes that time) but from a sense of a Gnostic as someone who could arrive at a tentative understanding that would be forever tenuous and, above all, be arrived at personally;**[23] **one person at a time; no doctrine.**

In talking about this subject over the years, I've found a fragile coalition of people who share certain points of view. We could never form a political party, or be a part of a lobbying group, or deliver a manifesto. It is a critical coalition whose efforts could lead to a more profound understanding of the nature of problems rather than of solutions.

In *Against the Current,* Isaiah Berlin[24] wrote a fascinating essay about Karl Marx. Berlin is speculative and circumspect. He doesn't insist on the rightness of the case he makes but says his analysis might contribute to a different perspective, another way of evaluating Marx. The subject is Marx's[25] well-known but often camouflaged anti-Semitism. Berlin speculated that Marx's painful experiences with an uncle who was a rabbi might have been an impetus toward his positing a society that was countryless and classless. In a sense, Marx might have been (unknowingly) prognosticating away the personal difficulties of his family as Jews, so that the source of his pain would disappear from history.

Similarly, Elias Canetti, in "Kafka's Other Trial," an essay in his book *The Conscience of Words,*[26] develops a hypothesis that associates Kafka and his peculiar relationships with several women (which Canetti surmised from reviewing Kafka's letters and diaries) with the subject matter of *The Trial.* Those private relationships interest me now, the associations between personal and artistic pieces of one's life.

Our contemporary paradigms are antiquated, our models parochial. In trying to understand the nature of problems, one has to come from fresh vantage points. Giambattista Vico, the Neapolitan philosopher of history, is innovative in terms of his speculations about time, what the term might mean in different historical periods, and how one might attempt to understand a time outside one's own. I could perhaps intuit your wife's perspective, and Count Cagliostro's skulduggery, and Akhenaton's[27] idea of God. It would be possible to move backward and forward, stopping at various stations, able to belong, to empathize with that moment. Vico's is a moving paradigm with laws internal to each historic moment.

Vico hypothesizes that one can actually jump over one's own predictable interests, and understand oneself from outside in as well as from inside out.

24. *Isaiah Berlin, cover of* Against the Current.
25. *Karl Marx, cover of* A World Without Jews.
26. *Elias Canetti, title page of* "Kafka's Other Trial."    27. *Bust of Akhenaton.*

Maybe both perspectives are necessary to produce a story. In other words, a narrative could be asymptotic to the truth. Instead of "no one can say," "someone might possibly say."

In that sense, it might be conceivable to approach an investigation of the relativity of vantage points like that of Akira Kurosawa's *Rashomon*[28] and understand what actually happened. The question in the film was "Could one look at a series of events  empirically and narrate the story, or was the perspective of the narrative always tied to the self-interest of the narrator?" I never felt that Kurosawa's conclusion was that one could never determine what actually had happened. Maybe there is no one who has the capacity to do it, who is empirically exacting *and* sufficiently disinterested. But theoretically it's conceivable. Not "there's no plausible single truth." And perhaps you could get closer to the truth. That would be a target. That doesn't mean you could represent the truth only by narrating the woman, the samurai, the bandit, the priest, all in a caricatured way, understand their interests and therefore their vantage points.[29] *Where is the suprapersonal narrative?*

*Rashomon*

If the avant-garde becomes a club—everybody sitting around congratulating one another on how sophisticated they are—then it becomes another established allegiance. I'm looking for a way to keep the internal discussion open. Which means I would continue to take my ideas, my instincts apart, and have the courage to do that. Individuals can advocate consistency. Cultures can pursue consistency. But finally consistency fractures under the pressure of conditions that can't ultimately be excluded. The alleged non sequitur is a sequitur after all. And a new (consistent) emphasis might be suggested for a time

Understanding is private first. There may be a time later when it can be shared.

In one way, the Gnostic sort of private advocacy feels terribly isolating. Each life buried in its own mystery, like the man who continues to plow the field and never pays attention to Icarus's fall in Brueghel's *Landscape with the Fall of Icarus*.[30] I'm not sure to what extent an external experience could free me from my own mystery, and allow me to see or understand in a more extroverted way. I have an interest in the possibility that something new could

28. Film still from Akira Kurosawa's Rashomon. *See also 3.26 and 3.32.*
29. Film still from Kurasawa's Rashomon: *"The Princess, the Samurai, and the Bandit."*   30. *See 3.12.*

happen—a fresh insight, whether the impetus is from inside or outside. It might never occur. It might rarely occur. I wouldn't want to say that it would necessarily occur. **Or perhaps it could occur by degree. But there is just the possibility that I could make explicit the problematic nature of what I can't make explicit.**

## AWARDS

Los Angeles Urban Beautification Award, 1998.

Los Angeles Business Journal, Best Commercial Building, 1998.

AIA/LA Honor Award, 1996.

Progressive Architecture Design Award, 1992.

## BOOKS/MONOGRAPHS

*New American Architects III.* Cologne: Taschen, June 1997.

Eric Owen Moss: *Buildings and Projects 2.* Introduction by Anthony Vidler. New York: Rizzoli International Publications, March 1996.

*Eric Owen Moss 1974-1994. a + u,* special issue, November, 1994.

*Eric Own Moss Academy Editions Monograph.* Academy Group Ltd., June 1993.

*Eric Owen Moss,* London: Academy Group Ltd., June 1993.

Eric Owen Moss: *Buildings and Projects 1,* Forward by Philip Johnson, Introduction by Wolf Prix, New York: Rizzoli International Publications, October 1991.

## SELECTED ARTICLES

Koch, Michael. "Eric Owen Moss: Gnostic Architecture," *Dialogue* (Taiwan) August 1997.

Chow, Phoebe. "Edge City Spectacle," *Architectural Review* (Great Britain) April 1997.

Beck, Haig. "Reviewing Eric Owen Moss," *UME* (Australia) April 1997.

Lavalou, Armelle. "Eric Owen Moss, Samitaur Building" *L'Architecture d'Aujourd'hui* (France) April, 1997.

Pitrowski, Christa. "Arbeiterkultur und Low-Tech-Futurismus," *Neue Zurcher Zeiting* (Switzerland) March 10, 1997.

Pidgeon, Monica and Young, Elizabeth. "The Urban Misfit," *Blueprint* (Great Britain) March 1997.

Dixon, John Morris. "Eric Owen Moss," *KA* (Korean Architects) February 1997.

Stephens, Suzanne. "The Samitaur Building," *Architectural Record,* February 1997.

"Rising Above It All," *Los Angeles Times,* November 10, 1996.

Ouroussoff, Nicolai. "The Latest Alteration of a City's Industrial Fabric," *Los Angeles Times,* October 26, 1996.

"The City of Culver City: A Paradigm for Change," *L'ARCA* (Italy) February 1996.

Muschamp, Herbert. "Lifting the Sights of a Neighborhood Tired and Low," *The New York Times,* October 1995.

Dixon, John Morris. "Process: Superstructure," *Progressive Architecture,* July 1995.

"Good Times Guide: Architecture," *Traveler's Journal: Los Angeles,* Fall 1994.

Muschamp, Herbert. "An Enterprise Zone for the Imagination," *New York Times,* Architecture Section, March 14, 1993.

*Progressive Architecture,* The 39th Annual P/A Awards, January 1992.

IMAGE GUIDE
SECTION 2:

# PHOTOGRAPHY CREDITS

## SECTION I

1.2 photo montage, Todd Conversano

1.5 Lawson/Westen House, Tom Bonner

1.8 Tom Bonner

1.12 Nick Tucker

All others courtesy of Eric Owen Moss Architects

## SECTION 2

2.1 > 2.2 Tom Bonner

2.3 Paul Groh

2.4 > 2.6 Tom Bonner

2.7 Paul Groh

2.8 > 2.10 Tom Bonner

2.11 Paul Groh

2.12 Tom Bonner

2.13 upper left: Paul Groh

      lower right: Tom Bonner

2.14 > 2.20 Tom Bonner

2.22 Nick Tucker

2.23 > 2.27 Tom Bonner

2.28 Paul Groh

2.29 > 2.30 Tom Bonner

2.31 Paul Groh

2.32 > 2.34 Tom Bonner

2.35 Paul Groh

2.36 > 2.37 Tom Bonner

2.38 > 2.40 Paul Groh

2.41 > 2.42 Tom Bonner

2.43 top: Tom Bonner

      middle: Paul Groh

## SECTION 3

3.23 *The Petal House*, Tim Street-Porter

All others courtesy of Eric Owen Moss Architects

## SECTION 4

4.3 Todd Conversano

4.7 Todd Conversano

4.28 Todd Conversano

All others Paul Groh

## SECTION 5

5:5 upper right, Paul Groh

All others courtesy of Eric Owen Moss Architects

# PROJECT CREDITS

## DESIGN
1989-1995

### PROJECT ARCHITECTS
Jay Vanos
Dennis Ige

### PROJECT TEAM
Mark Prezkop
Todd Conversano
Greg Baker
John Bencher
David Wick
Eric Holmquist
Paul Groh
Naoto Sekiguchi
Ravindran Kodalur Subramanian
Scott Nakao
Elissa Scrafano
Scott Hunter
Sophie Harvey
Sheng Yuan-Hwang
Isabel Duvivier
Carol Hove
Karin Mahle
Daryusch Sepehr
Ann Bergren
Jennifer Rakow
Amanda Hyde
Lucas Rios
Eduoardo Sabater
Janek Tabencki Dombrowa
Leticia S. Lau
Erik Hohberger
Julia Burbach

### STRUCTURAL ENGINEER
Joe Kurily
*Kurily Szymanski Tchirkow*

### MECHANICAL ENGINEER
Paul Antieri
*I & N Consulting Engineers*

### ELECTRICAL ENGINEER
Paul Immerman
*I & N Consulting Engineers*

### LIGHTING CONSULTANT
Saul Goldin
*Saul Goldin and Associates*

### CONSTRUCTION
*Samitaur Constructs*
Supervisors
  Peter Brown, *Director of Field Operations*
  Tim Brown, *Superintendent*

### PHOTOGRAPHER
Tom Bonner